WHAT OTHERS ARE SAYING ABOUT THIS BOOK:

"Great reading! ***Communicating with Deaf Children*** *provides an excellent summary of communication issues related to teaching deaf children. Parents, candidates in teacher training programs for the deaf and hard of hearing as well as current educators will gain additional insight about the methods teaching professionals have struggled with for so many years."*

-Jan Jones-Wadsworth, EdD, Consultant,
CALIFORNIA COMMISSION ON TEACHER CREDENTIALING

"Editor Tom Bertling has provided an intriguing collection of essays that are not easily found elsewhere. Students, parents, and professionals alike from all political viewpoints will be quite pleased at the wealth of information made readily available from various people of experience.

Logic dictates that for a truly fair decision to be made one must look at all sides of the issue. American Sign Language (ASL) is a beautiful expressive language that certainly has its merits, and publications from other experts on anASL-orientated education can be found. The counterpoint to them is provided by this book, thus ensuring a justified balance. Bertling has given us a refreshing look at the furor encompassing the war of propagandists that is oft known as deaf politics."

-G. James Bland, Student, Tutor, ASL Instr.
COLORADO

COMMUNICATING WITH DEAF CHILDREN

"I appreciate the diverse perspectives of instructional methodologies, communication modalities and the application of technology in the education of deaf and hard of hearing children. Parents need to be well informed about educational opportunities for their children with hearing loss, but, more importantly, they need to be open-minded and flexible about meeting their child's needs."

-Dr. T. Alan Hurwitz, Dean
NAT'L TECH. INST. FOR THE DEAF AT ROCHESTER INST. OF TECHNOLOGY

*"**Communicating with Deaf Children** is an excellent resource for people who want to contribute to the language development of children with hearing disabilities. Proper language development is a necessity for people, disabled or not, to achieve safety, good health and self sufficiency"*

-Richard Roehm, Chief Executive Officer
ORANGE CO. DEAF ADVOCACY CTR.

"As a deaf person of hearing parents, an educator, professor and lecturer at schools for the deaf around the world, and a recent cochlear implantee, I am of the opinion the future of deaf education lies with the CI. This book provides educators with clear and straightforward choices to enable all deaf children an equal chance to achieve English literacy."

-Professor Frances M. Parsons, Author
***GALLAUDET UNIVERSITY** (Retired)*

COMMUNICATING WITH DEAF CHILDREN

*"**Communicating with Deaf Children** brings to parents, educators, administrators and interested persons with hearing loss important awareness of what is really vital in communcating with deaf and hard of hearing children. This book confirms that English cannot be ignored as the primary language for children if they are to succeed. Information on cochlear implants, cued speech, Sign Coded English, and captioned media, all of which I'm an advocate for, are presented in this convincing book aimed at ensuring English literacy in our deaf children."*

-Bruce Gross, Educator of the Deaf/HOH
L.A. COUNTY OFFICE OF EDUCATION

"Parents and professionals who are stymied by the controversy of communcation approaches for deaf children can turn to Tom Bertling's comprehensive update on cochlear implants, Cued Speech and Coded English. All contributions in the book guide the reader towards making decisions that help provide the deaf child with working tools for using English in both the hearing and deaf communities."

-Edward Scouten, Distinguished Educator
NTID/GALLAUDET UNIVERSITY

*"**Communicating with Deaf Children** is great reading, covering from A to Z the very complex communication issues faced by their parents and educators working with these children. Administrators of deaf and hard of hearing programs should absorb this book, become familiar with the views expressed by its contributors, and have as part of their repertoire when responding to parents who question a placement decision."*

-Steve Longacre, Principal, D/HH Program
TAFT ELEM. SCHOOL, SANTA ANA, CA

COMMUNICATING WITH DEAF CHILDREN

EDITOR'S NOTE:

Notes of appreciation go to Frank Bowe, Paulette Caswell, Melissa Chaikof, Dena Davis, Poala Costa Giovangigli, Gerilee Gustason, John Hopkins University Press, Glenn Lloyd, Frances Parsons, Patrick Seamans and Mardie Younglof. Special thanks to Valerie Jo and Rikki Sage as always.

PUBLISHER'S NOTE:

The opinions voiced by the contributors to this book are theirs alone and do not necessarily reflect those held by the publisher or the publishing company. We do support one's right to express an opinion and we stand behind all our writers in this regard. We strongly support our society's intolerance for censorship and wholly oppose any attempt to impose restrictions on our rights to free speech and freedom of the press.

There is very little agreement among all the factions involved in the education of the deaf child. Parents must explore all possibilities and options, then make the best decision for ***their*** *child.*

It is not our intent to identify or ridicule anyone personally in this book. Only individuals who have already publicly spoken out or have become part of the published public record may have been identified.

KODIAK MEDIA GROUP:

Publishers of vital educational and scholastic material. Available domestically and worldwide through most major school and library book wholesalers and distributors, Internet book websites, or you may contact the publisher directly. Large quantity educational discounts available.

COMMUNICATING WITH DEAF CHILDREN

FRANK BOWE

PAULETTE CASWELL

MELISSA CHAIKOF

DENA DAVIS

GERILEE GUSTASON

GLENN LLOYD

PATRICK SEAMANS

Edited by TOM BERTLING

KODIAK MEDIA GROUP

COMMUNICATING WITH DEAF CHILDREN

First edition published 2002

10 9 8 7 6 5 4 3 2 1

For further information contact: KODIAK MEDIA GROUP
P.O. Box 1029-B5
Wilsonville, Oregon 97070

SAN: 297.9993

ISBN: 0-9637813-8-3

U.S. Library of Congress Catalog Card Number: 2002101157

PUBLISHER'S CATALOGING IN PUBLICATION DATA:
Edited by Tom Bertling.
Communicating with Deaf Children.
Bibliography information.
1. Deafness--United States. 2. Deaf--Education of deaf children.
3. Deaf--Means of communication. 4. Sign Language and
Linguistics. 5. Cultural issues. 6. Cochlear implants. I Title.

Kodiak Media Group is a privately owned company and receives no private or public (including non-profit) special-interest funding or grants.

comchild02

CONTENTS

COMMUNICATING WITH DEAF CHILDREN

TO THE READERS:

Many professionals are confused about the true difference between American Sign Language (ASL) and Sign-Coded English (SCE). The ASL LANGUAGE is not based on the sounds of speech. It conveys information PURELY through gestures, body positions, and facial expressions. It is a purely visual-gestural-mimetic language. SCE is the use of the ASL signs to assist with lipreading of the English language, with the signs matching the lipread English language to give the general meaning of the main words in the sentences being lipread.

Here are some examples. Since ASL cannot be written or spoken, only the text equivalents of this language are interpreted below.

SCE: Let me give you one example.
ASL: Me now show-you.

SCE: I love my mother.
ASL: My mother me love.

SCE: I can't find my glasses.
ASL: Glasses mine. Find can't.

SCE: My boss will fire me if I telephone (in) sick again.
ASL: If maybe me telephone boss sick again happen what? Fire will.

SCE: ASL has (a) variety of rules and different grammar structure(s).
ASL: ASL specific have different different rule different different grammar different different structure.

ASL does not convey the complete precision of the meaning of the English words and sentences, particularly in higher level English sentences. This difference is most apparent when the words and sentences are above the usual 4th grade level of United States academic instruction. SCE does convey complete precision of the English words, sentences, and language structure, since it is based on lipread information, supplemented by ASL signs to denote general meaning.

[Thanks to Dr. Paulette Caswell. Source of examples: the videotape created by Dr. Nathie Marbury, which is distributed through the National Association of the Deaf (NAD) video distribution services division.]

CHAPTER ONE

COCHLEAR IMPLANTS AND THE CLAIMS OF CULTURE? A RESPONSE TO LANE AND GRODIN

by Dena S. Davis, JD, PhD

[Dena S. Davis, is hearing and an Associate Professor of Law at Cleveland-Marshall College of Law, Cleveland State University. His essay is a rebuttal to the claims made in a paper (see reference section) authored by Harlan Lane and Michael Grodin. (Lane is an advocate of Deaf culture and American Sign Language (ASL) and an opponent of implanting deaf children with the cochlear implant).]

ABSTRACT: Because I reject the notion physical characteristics constitute cultural membership, I argue that, even if the claim were persuasive that deafness is a culture rather than a disability, there is no reason to fault hearing parents who choose cochlear implants for their deaf children.

Let me begin by expressing my gratitude to Harlan Lane and Michael Grodin (1997) for their provocative and hard-hitting article. By positing a situation in which cochlear implants are risk-free and effective, they have constructed the strongest case possible for the use of such implants and thus have challenged themselves to make the most robust and uncompromising argument for the position that DEAF *[here, the capitalized word "DEAF" generally refers to the small minority of deaf individuals who support the usage of ASL and believe in the existence of a deaf culture]* people are not disabled, but, rather, are members of a linguistic/cultural minority, and that parents act wrongly when they seek to convert deaf babies into hearing ones. I will respond under three headings.

IS DEAFNESS A DISABILITY?

I cannot accept the claim that deafness is not to be perceived as a disability. The DEAF-WORLD of which the authors speak has created a rich and unique culture, and I am happy to assent to the claim that culture is qualitatively, though not quantitatively, equal to that of the hearing world. It also is true that a great deal of what "disables" the deaf in our present world is socially constructed and could be substantially ameliorated by a more caring majority. But there is a difference between valuing the culture that the DEAF-WORLD has built and equating deafness *with* culture.

One of the defining differences between culture and disability is the option that human adults have to choose the extent to which they identify with and participate in their culture. As the authors state, many people who are physically deaf are not members of the DEAF-WORLD (p. 233). Some hearing people are more at home in the DEAF-WORLD and more fluent in American Sign Language (ASL) than are many deaf people (Cohen, 1995). Despite the many positive aspects of the DEAF-WORLD and despite the fact that DEAF and deaf people may, on average, lead lives as happy and productive as those of hearing people, I maintain that the inability to hear is a deficit, a disability, a lack of perfect health. A hearing person has a *choice* about whether to participate in DEAF culture, by learning ASL, attending social and cultural events, and so on. A nonhearing person, however, is *irrevocably cut off* from large areas of the hearing world. Even if I were to follow Lane and Grodin's generous example and posit an ideal educational environment for the deaf, most prelingually deafened persons would not be able to communicate effectively orally, with obvious social and vocational consequences. (I can anticipate an obvious response, that hearing people are equally disadvantaged because they can never be fully accepted in the DEAF-WORLD. But if that is true, it is because DEAF people are prejudiced against them, not because they are unable to learn the necessary skills.)

IS CULTURAL MEMBERSHIP PHYSIOLOGICALLY DETERMINED?

I reject the notion that physical characteristics, hereditary or congenital, constitute cultural membership. Culture, the "body of customary beliefs, social forms, and material traits constituting a distinct complex of tradition of a racial, religious, or social group" (Webster's International Dictionary, 1993), is passed on by people, not by genes. A child born into an Ashkenazic Jewish family, for example, partakes of that culture because her parents pass it on to her, *in exactly the same way* as they would pass it on to a child whom they adopted at birth (or as an embryo). Should this couple happen to have both a biological child and an adopted one, they would not consider one child to be "more" Jewish than the other. This is as silly as saying that [former Secretary of State] Madeleine Albright is "really" Jewish. The opposite notion seems to me deeply racist and genetically determinist.

There are, of course, some counter examples to my claim, as Lane and Grodin point out. In one type of counter example, one acknowledges that a white couple raising an African-American child has an obligation to give the child a clear and proud sense of her black identity because, whatever they do, the child will be treated by others as a black person and therefore she needs a proud racial identity as a buffer against racism. In another type of counter example, one might argue that a child of Italian descent should know something about his parents' and grandparents' culture, feel proud of the accomplishments of his ancestors, and so forth. But neither of these arguments fits the situation of a deaf child born to hearing parents. Many deaf children who are fitted with cochlear implants will not be treated by others as deaf, and children of hearing parents obviously do not have deaf ancestors. *[In rare cases it is possible to have deaf grandparents or great-grandparents.]*

My point is that even if I were to accept the claim that deafness is a culture rather than a disability and even if there were *no* downsides to being deaf, there is no reason to fault hearing parents who, reasonably enough, prefer to have children who share their language and culture -- and those of their siblings -- and who do not require huge investments of parental resources to learn sign language, to pay for special schools and equipment, and so on.

PRESERVATION OF MINORITY CULTURES

Lane and Grodin raise the question of whether, since the "preservation of minority cultures is a good," parents have an ethical obligation not to choose cochlear implants for their nonhearing child, because converting their child from deaf -- and therefore potentially DEAF -- to hearing diminishes the population strength of the DEAF-WORLD. I perceive three arguments against this claim.

First, even if deafness is a culture rather than a disability, I think that the authors are, quite simply, asking too much. Raising a DEAF child well requires an enormous commitment of time, money, and energy. Parents, who usually are not expecting their new baby to be deaf, must learn ASL quickly in order to communicate with their child early so that language is mastered at the appropriate developmental stages. In addition, they may need to pull up stakes and relocate to a community that can offer the appropriate services. If they adopt the DEAF values that the authors describe, integration of their child into hearing schools will be "anathema," and they probably will have to send their child to a residential school at a much earlier age than they would normally contemplate. If cochlear implants in the first year of life present a risk-free alternative, it seems unrealistic to expect parents to choose this enormous burden for reasons unrelated to the welfare of their child. (Especially since, as the authors suggest, it is not wrong to seek to cure such deafness-causing diseases as meningitis even if doing so will reduce the DEAF population.) Furthermore, hearing parents might plausibly worry that they will not be successful in raising a happy and productive DEAF or deaf child; how much simpler, then, from the perspective of the child's own well-being, to choose the implant.

Second, as the authors point out, there are many more "deaf" people *[generally, they are deaf people who do not use ASL or belong to, or believe in, a deaf culture]* than there are "DEAF" people since many "visual" people fail to become successful members of the DEAF-WORLD or choose not to do so. Thus, there is no certainty, perhaps not even a likelihood, that the child in question will make that step, and without that likelihood all of the arguments about not diminishing minority cultures fall flat.

Third, against the authors' positive depiction of the DEAF-WORLD, one needs to think seriously about the limited opportunities that exist for even the most positively acculturated DEAF people. Marriage partners, conversation partners, vocations, and avocations are severely limited. Yes, one can think of cultural minorities about whom the same could be said -- e.g., the Amish or ultra Orthodox Jews -- but these children can change their minds as adults and a significant percentage do so. As I have argued elsewhere, every child has a "right to an open future" (Davis, 1997; the concept is Joel Feinberg's) in which she can choose her mate, her vocation, her religion, her reading material, her place of residence, and so forth. Because deafness severely limits the child's future *in an irrevocable fashion,* I cannot agree that parents act wrongly in "curing" a child's deafness.[1] Furthermore, if deafness is not a culture but a disability, then the authors' claim becomes even harder to sustain, even if that disability were the entry ticket to a rich and happy culture.

Against these arguments, the authors suggest that the parents of a deaf child have a special connection to the DEAF-WORLD, which grounds a unique obligation to be concerned for the continuing strength and flourishing of the DEAF population. They suggest that this special concern may be powerful enough to tip the balance when parents are weighing their obligations to the child's best interest against their moral concern for the flourishing of minority cultures. This suggestion seems false. We all have obligations to be concerned about the situation of vulnerable minorities. Those of us in the majority group who have family members in the minority population arguably have a special awareness of the minority situation, but not therefore a unique obligation. It is not, after all, considered a valid moral argument to say, "Why should I care about the flourishing of the DEAF population? No one in my family is DEAF!" Some years ago, when my only child was quite young, I would occasionally -- mostly to be provocative -- respond to persons who questioned my active commitment to gay rights by saying that, after all, my son had approximately a 10 percent chance of turning out to be gay, and I needed to enhance his chances of having a just and pro-gay society to live in. But in retrospect, that seems nonsensical; now that my child has turned out to be heterosexual, I certainly do not think that I have any less reason to continue my work for gay rights.

In conclusion, I cannot accept the foundational claim tha deafness is primarily to be understood as (potential) membership in a cultural and linguistic minority, rather than as a disability. But even if I were to be persuaded to that claim, I do not agree that the needs of that culture for continuing population strength trump a hearing family's plausible assumption that, by giving their baby improved hearing, they have increased her chances for a happy life and also for a much more open future.

Like the authors, I end with more questions. By limiting myself to Lane and Grodin's challenge, I have made only a very narrow claim: that hearing parents do not act wrongly when they choose a (safe and effective) cochlear implant for a deaf baby. Questions abound for future dialogue: Do hearing parents therefore act wrongly if they *decide against* an implant? Ought this to be considered neglect and grounds for the state to step in and insist on an implant? What about parents who are deaf or DEAF? Is it wrong for them to choose an implant for their children? Wrong for them to refuse an implant? Wrong for them to seek genetic counseling to maximize their chances of having deaf children? Wrong for them deliberately to expose themselves to rubella, for example, in order to change a hearing fetus to a deaf one? If we accept the disability premise, these will be tough questions with which to grapple.

NOTE:

1.) Lane and Grodin note that most DEAF adults are opposed to the notion of cochlear implants and infer from that DEAF children would refuse implant surgery if they were old enough to be consulted. But, of course, in my view, children are not born DEAF, merely deaf. Further, it makes as much sense to ask ordinary hearing people now if they would have wanted implants had they been born deaf as it does to ask DEAF people that question.

REFERENCES:

Cohen, Leah. 1995. *Train Go Sorry: Inside a Deaf World*. Boston: Houghton Mifflin.

Davis, Dena S. 1997. Genetic Dilemmas and the Child's Right to an Open Future. *Hastings Center Report* 27 (2):7-15.

Lane, Harlan, and Grodin, Michael. 1997. Ethical Issues in Cochlear Implant Surgery: An Exploration into Disease, Disability, and the Best Interests of the Child. *Kennedy Institute of Ethics Journal* 7: 231-51.

CHAPTER TWO

ENGLISH LANGUAGE ACQUISITION OF CHILDREN WITH COCHLEAR IMPLANTS

by Melissa K. Chaikof

[Melissa K. Chaikof received her B.A. from the University of Pennsylvania and her M.S. from Johns Hopkins University. She has been an associate editor of Cochlear Implant Assoc.'s CONTACT publication since 1996 and served on the Board of the Auditory-Verbal Center of Atlanta for six years, five of those as an officer. Two of Melissa's three children hear with a cochlear implant. The oldest received hers in 1989 at age two. The youngest received hers in 1996 at age 15 months.]

In 1990, the FDA approved the first multi-channel cochlear implant (CI) for children ages two and older. Since then, because this device enables so many more deaf children to hear spoken language and master oral communication, the field of deafness has been evolving at a very rapid pace. In his book, *Cochlear Implants for Kids,*[1] Warren Estabrooks states,

> "Never before in the history of the education of children who are deaf has there been such potential for *listening*. For many children who are unable to learn to hear and listen with hearing aids, cochlear implants can provide access to a world rich in sound and spoken language. Through consistent cochlear implant management and systematic auditory (re)habilitation (listening therapy) with maximum parental involvement, these children

learn to listen to their own voices, the voices of others, and the sounds of the environment in order to communicate using speech."

The multi-channel CI provides a young profoundly deaf child with the potential to learn to listen and to discriminate sound well enough to be able to comprehend spoken language auditorially and to learn to speak well. However, the CI is only a tool that will help a child achieve this goal. Normal hearing children learn to comprehend language and speak through their hearing. It stands to reason that, the better a hearing impaired child can hear and understand through an auditory channel, the easier a time they will have learning language, and their progress will more closely resemble that of a hearing child's. Such has been the situation with hearing-impaired children utilizing acoustic amplification: auditory comprehension and expressive language are improved by listening-speaking therapy. A child with a CI ("electric hearing") may similarly benefit from listening-speaking therapy.

Findings from a study by Robbins, Svirsky and Kirk (1997)[2] confirm this. They compared two groups of children, those who were deaf and did not have CIs and those who were deaf and received Nucleus 22 CIs. They found that, while the English language skills of the children without CIs improved at a rate that was markedly lower than that of their normal hearing peers, those with implants had progressed after one year of implant use at a rate that was seven months greater than those without implants. The authors concluded that the CI promoted development of receptive and expressive language.

With the rapid increase in the number of young children with CIs, the debate over what factors most influence English language acquisition in these children has attracted increased interest. To date, research has identified two major factors: age of implantation and educational approach to teaching language.

AGE AT COCHLEAR IMPLANTATION

Neurologists have long known that the critical years for learning language and for learning to make sense of auditory input are the first two to three of a child's life. These are the years when the brain is most plastic.[3] Arthur Boothroyd, Professor of Speech and Hearing Services at the City University of New York, writes in his book, *Hearing Impairments in Young Children*,[4] that, "There is compelling evidence to suggest that children are neurologically ready to acquire basic perceptual skills and language skills during the first few years of life and that if advantage is not taken of this readiness, there may be irreversible neurological changes that interfere with learning at a later age." In addition, early implantation decreases the period of auditory deprivation for deaf children and, thus, gives them more time during their preschool years to close their language gap.[5]

Sharma, Dorman, Spahr, and Tod[6] confirmed the existence of this critical period when they investigated the period of time in which the human auditory system remains nondegenerate or plastic in congenitally deafened children. By measuring auditory evoked cortical N1-P1 potentials to speech sounds (baa baa baa baa baa . . .) in congenitally deafened children with CIs, they determined that the children implanted by age three displayed normal responses within months of implant activation, whereas children implanted at age four or older had abnormal responses, even after years of hearing with their implants.

Knowledge of this critical window for learning language has provided the impetus both for state-run early intervention programs and for more recent efforts to pass legislation both at the state and national level mandating universal newborn hearing screening. Thus, it makes sense that the earlier a profoundly deaf child receives a CI and is able to begin hearing, the better their performance with that CI will be.

Waltzman, Cohen, Gomolin, Shapiro, Ozdamar, and Hoffman (1994)[7] conducted one of the earlier studies on English language acquisition in relation to early implantation. At the time, with FDA guidelines still stipulating a minimum age of implantation of two years, they examined a group of oral/aural children implanted before the age of three and concluded that early implantation is beneficial to the development of auditory perceptual skills. However, they also make the point that, in addition to early implantation, this group of children had received certain benefits from participation in the study including skilled and frequent programming of the implant processor, an appropriate educational setting, and parental involvement. Brackett and Zara conducted a similar study (1998)[8] in which they concluded that children implanted before age five, but particularly before age three, achieved improved performance in English language acquisition.

Both of these studies were conducted when the youngest FDA-approved age for implantation was two years. More recently, for at least one CI brand, the FDA-approved age has been lowered to 12 months. A study by Mario A. Svirsky, PhD,[9] from the Indiana Univ. School of Medicine, found that the younger a profoundly deaf child is at implantation, the more likely speech development and perception will coincide with chronological age. All the children in this study showed a gap between their language age and their chronological age, but the gap was wider for older children. Language perception and verbal skills in the children with CIs showed impressive accomplishments, and the gap between hearing children and children with CIs continued to narrow as time passed after implantation. According to Dr. Svirsky,

> "The rate of language development in the profoundly deaf children after implantation was quite close to that of children with normal hearing, and it exceeded the development rate expected from unimplanted profoundly deaf children. . . . Some children in the experimental group showed above-average rates of language acquisition and achieved scores that were comparable to those of their hearing peers after only 2.5 years of using their CI."

Finally, the most recent study from the University of Michigan[10] states that, "The younger deaf and hearing-impaired children are when a CI awakens their hearing, the better they will do on speech recognition tests later in life." They found a significant difference in speech recognition between those who received their CIs between two and four years of age, during the critical language development period, compared to those who received them later. The Michigan team is still researching the benefits of implantation before age two, as this is still a fairly new development, but concludes from their results thus far that these patients are already showing a difference in performance over those who received their implants at a later age.

EDUCATIONAL APPROACHES TO TEACHING LANGUAGE

Once a young child has a CI, the next crucial factor in English language acquisition is educational approach. The best approach to teaching a hearing impaired child language has always been one of the most controversial and heated topics. Whereas before the advent of the CI, arguments against an oral approach resulted from the difficulties in learning spoken English without the benefit of hearing, now the situation has changed greatly, since the implant provides substantial enough hearing to make this a much less arduous process.

Yet, the debate continues, in fact as heated as ever. While CIs in children as young as age two have been FDA-approved since 1990, it is only recently that the number of children using a CI for a significant period of time is enough to measure results. Furthermore, for most of the time that the implant has existed, proponents of ASL approaches were, for the most part, members of the deaf culture who vehemently opposed CIs in young children. It has only been recently that some in this group have recognized the value of CIs and, instead of opposing them, have begun to attempt to work with these children, although still insisting on maintaining a predominantly ASL-based approach to teaching language.

Most notable among the ASL deaf community's burgeoning acceptance of the CI in young children is Gallaudet University's recently opened Cochlear Implant Education Center. Their school information[11] contains the following:

> "The goal of CI technology is to provide deaf children with increased access to sound. An important focus for students with implants is, therefore, to maximize this access to sound toward the development and use of spoken English. We equally believe that students with CIs should be provided with the opportunity to develop skill in ASL and knowledge of Deaf culture."

With some in the ASL deaf community now jumping on the CI bandwagon, the question arises a to whether or not a manual approach to teaching these children language will afford them the same opportunities to acquire high levels of auditory perception and spoken language attained by their peers in more oral programs. Furthermore, do children in Total Communication (TC) programs, where the emphasis on the auditory is nowhere near as substantial as in oral and, in particular, Auditory-Verbal (A-V) programs, attain similar levels of auditory comprehension and mastery of spoken English? Much of the research has centered on language acquisition, meaning that children were tested in whatever communication mode they used. Thus, specific measures of levels of spoken English language were not apparent. More recent studies, though, have examined this issue.

Most of the studies have focused on an oral vs. a TC approach. However, a few have looked at an ASL-based approach, and a few recent studies are separating the oral group into auditory-oral -- that is an approach that emphasizes both auditory information and speechreading and is often practiced in a self-contained classroom -- and A-V, which emphasizes only the auditory and is thus the most auditory of approaches and which advocates mainstreaming.

Rose, Vernon and Pool (1996)[12] conducted an early study involving children with CIs. In a study of 45 residential and day schools for the deaf, which were comprised of ASL, TC, and oral programs, they found that, of 151 implanted children, 71, or 47%, were no longer using their CIs. However, of those who were continuing to use their implants, 65% were clustered into three programs, two of which were strictly oral and the third of which was a state school that had incorporated a strong oral program. Estabrooks and Mordica (2000)[13] studied CI students living in and around a metropolitan area in order to determine their functional communication skills with their CI. These students attended either an oral day school, a TC day school, or a residential school. Their findings indicated correlates for non-use of the CI to be (1) use of sign language in the home and at school, (2) a rural address, and (3) known etiology of hearing loss, such as hereditary or other with associated potential learning disabilities and attention issues.

Most of the literature examining effect of communication approach on English-language acquisition considers only two approaches, oral and TC. Osberger, Zimmerman-Phillips, and Fisher (1997),[14] in a study of the relationship between communication mode and CI performance in pediatric Clarion CI patients found that the mean scores on a standard battery of tests of those children who used an oral approach were significantly higher on all tests than those who used TC. In addition, they found that the oral children demonstrated a much faster rate of auditory learning with their CIs than did the TC children.

Young, Grohne, Carrasco, and Brown (2000)[15] performed a similar study and found similar results. Children in their study who used oral communication acquired auditory perception skills with their CIs at a more rapid rate than the TC children in the short term (six months). However, differing from the other studies, they also found that the TC group were able to make up that difference in the long term (12 months).

The University of Miami Ear Institute CI team has done a few studies examining speech perception and linguistic abilities of young CI children. Hodges, Ash, Balkany, Schloffman, and Butts (1999)[16] studied factors that contribute to speech perception abilities in these children. They noted a wide variance in performance outcomes among children in their group. To examine the reasons for these differences, they considered the following factors: length of CI use, age at surgery, device type, socioeconomic status (SES), bilingualism, school setting, and participation in private therapy. All speech perception testing was completely auditory. Of the 40 children studied, 21 used TC and 19 used oral communication, including 12 who received private therapy from a certified A-V therapist. They found that those children who used some form of oral communication scored significantly higher on both closed and open set tests of speech perception.

While the authors determined that the strongest variable contributing to performance difference was communication mode, they also found that children in higher SES groups, those who attended private schools, and those who received private therapy also performed better. As they point out, children in higher SES groups are also the ones who are more likely to attend private schools and receive private therapy. In addition, they point out that children from middle and lower SES groups are more likely dependent upon the public schools for all educational services, and most public school programs represented in their study were TC. They also note that the two children in public school oral programs scored above the TC group mean on all speech measures. In addition, one oral child in a lower SES group scored not only above the TC group mean but also well above the oral group mean. Of all the children in a higher SES group, the mean score for the oral children was substantially higher than that for the TC children. The authors conclude that SES alone does not account for differences in speech perception abilities.

In another University of Miami Ear Institute study, Cullington, Hodges, Butts, Dolan-Ash, and Balkany (2000)[17] compared the linguistic abilities of young CI recipients, all but one of whom were prelingually deafened. They found that, on a test of expressive vocabulary, the oral children demonstrated significantly less language delay than the TC. While the oral children also performed better on the other tests, these results were not statistically significant. The other interesting factor in this study, though, was that, despite scoring lower, the TC children had been using their CIs for significantly longer than those children in the oral group. The authors conclude that, while further research is needed, orally educated CI children achieve better language skills than those in TC programs.

Perhaps the most comprehensive study to date is that by Geers, Brenner, Nicholas, Uchanski, and Tye-Murray performed at the Center for Applied Research on Childhood Deafness at the Central Institute for the Deaf and funded by the United States National Institutes of Health.[18] They measured performance on a battery of tests for a sample of 180 eight- and nine-year-old prelingually deaf children implanted before age five, all of whom used the Nucleus 22 CI. The purpose of the study was to determine the "effects of various educational and rehabilitation models on the deaf child's ability to understand, produce and read English while using a Nucleus 22 CI." Measured outcomes included receptive and expressive language, auditory speech perception, speech intelligibility, reading comprehension, and social-emotional adjustment. Factors considered were communication mode used in class and therapy, ranging from a mostly sign TC program through oral to A-V, including number of hours of therapy, plus therapist experience, type of class placement, and parent participation in therapy. Also taken into account were intervening variables consisting of IQ, family characteristics including size of family and education and income, age of onset of deafness and at implantation, and map characteristics. The results of the research indicated that, while half the variance in skill level could be attributed to intervening variables associated with the CI, particularly IQ, significant additional variance could be attributed to rehabilitation factors, in particular to communication mode.

"Use of an oral communication mode contributed significant variance to all outcomes except for spoken and signed language. The greater the emphasis on speech and auditory skill development the better the outcome. Type of classroom reflects amount of time spent in a mainstream class. This variable was significant for speech production, language and reading.

". . . Children whose educational program emphasized dependence on speech and audition for communication were better able to use the information provided by the implant to hear, speak and read. Use of sign communication with implanted children did not promote auditory and speech skill development and did not result in an advantage for overall English language competence even when the outcome measure included sign language. Oral education appears to be an important educational choice for children who have received a CI before 5 years of age."

In the book *Choices in Deafness,*[19] Warren Estabrooks, Certified A-V Therapist, writes, "Recent scientific advances in amplification and CI technology have provided great potential listening opportunities for children all over the world. The A-V Approach is a natural companion of such technology."

The A-V approach differs from other approaches to teaching hearing impaired children language in that hearing, rather than vision, is emphasized. A-V children acquire language naturally through listening as do normally hearing children because they are taught to learn to listen and to maximize the use of either their residual hearing or their hearing obtained through a CI. In addition, these children attend mainstream schools so that they are immersed in a spoken-English environment throughout the day and are surrounded by the good speech and language role models of their normally hearing peers.

Because the CI provides deaf children with so much usable hearing, the A-V approach is an excellent match for a CI child as, working together, the A-V therapist and parents teach the child to understand spoken language through the auditory channel to as great an extent as possible. However, while many case histories and anecdotal stories exist that demonstrate not only the efficacy of this approach with CIs but also the tremendously successful results obtained, professional research is lagging behind, and thus a dearth of relevant papers on this topic exists.

Rhoades and Chisolm (2000)[20] describe the performance of young A-V children with CIs. While the study included some hearing aid users, a substantial number, 38%, of the 40 children in the study had implants from the start of the study, and another 30% transitioned from hearing aids to cochlear implants during the study. All participants in the study received intensive A-V (re)habilitation over a period of one to four years. Performance measures of the 14 "graduates" of the program indicated that they had closed the gap between their chronological ages and their language ages. That is, they attained language levels commensurate with their normally hearing peers. In three out of the four years of the study, they made greater than one year's progress in English-language acquisition to accomplish this level of progress.

Cochlear implantation of young children is a dynamic and evolving field. With competition between CI manufacturers spurring the race for ever better technology and with age of implantation lowering, the future for young deaf children is brighter. Corresponding to this rapid rise in technology is an equally rapid change in the field of deaf education. While there may not be an exactly right way to educate every CI child, education must focus on auditory training in order to teach these children to tap into the information from the implant so they can realize their maximum potential to understand and speak English.

While this field is still too new to determine whether an auditory-oral or A-V approach is ultimately superior, what is evident is that traditional oral programs, which previously relied heavily on lipreading, are now evolving to include more and more of the techniques used in A-V therapy. Chances are that, as those employing a traditional oral approach continue to emphasize the auditory more because this is now possible with the CI, children will be entering the mainstream at increasingly younger ages, as is also already occurring, and the two approaches will either merge into one or closely approach such a merger.

REFERENCES:

1. Estabrooks, Warren, ed., Cochlear Implants for Kids, Washington, DC, Alexander Graham Bell Association for the Deaf, 1998.
2. Robbins, AM, Svirsky, M, Kirk, KI. *Children with implants can speak, but can they communicate?* Otolaryngology - Head and Neck Surgery 1997; 117:155-60.
3. Hermann, BS, *Current diagnostics and office practice: Perspectives and implications of early identification of hearing loss.* Current Science 1994; 449-53.
4. Boothroyd, Arthur, Hearing Impairments in Young Children, Washington, DC, Alexander Graham Bell Assoc. for the Deaf, 1988.
5. Bollard, PM, Chute, PM, Popp, A, Parisier, SC, *Specific language growth in young children using the Clarion CI.* Annals of Oto-, Rhino- & Laryngology 1999; 108 (Suppl 177):119-23.
6. Sharma, A, Dorman, M, Spahr, A, Todd, W, *Early cochlear implantation in children allows normal development of cortical auditory pathways.* Presented at 8th Symposium Cochlear Implants in Children, Los Angeles, CA, February 28-March 3, 2001.
7. Waltzman, SB, Cohen, NL, Gomolin, RH, Shapiro, WH, Ozdamar, SR, Hoffman, RA, *Long-term results of early cochlear implantation in congenitally and prelingually deafened children.* The American Journal of Otology 1994; 15(Suppl 2):9-13.
8. Brackett, D, Zara, CV, *Communication outcomes related to early implantation.* The American Journal of Otology 1998; 19:453-460.
9. http://www.medicine.indiana.edu/news_releases/archive_

00/msvirsky_00.htm

10. Kileny, P, Zwolan, T, Ashbaugh, C, *Influence of age at implantation on performance with a cochlear implant in children.* Journal of Otology and Neurotology, 2001; 22:? --- or http://www.aamc.org/newsroom/bulletin/umich/010102.htm
11. Gallaudet University website http://clerccenter.gallaudet.edu/CIEC/
12. Rose, DE, Vernon, M, Pool, AF, *Cochlear implants in prelingually deaf children.* American Annals of the Deaf 1996; 141: 258-61.
13. Easterbrooks, SR, Mordica, JA, *Teachers' ratings of functional communication in students with cochlear implants.* American Annals of the Deaf 2000; 145:54-59.
14. Osberger, MJ, Zimmerman-Phillips, S, Fisher L, *Relationship between communication mode and implant performance in pediatric Clarion patients.* Presented at the Vth International Cochlear Implant Conference, New York, NY, May 1-3, 1997.
15. Young, NM, Grohne, KM, Carrasco, VN, Brown CJ, *Speech perception in young children using Nucleus or Clarion cochlear implants: effect of communication mode.* Proceedings of Seventh Symposium on CIs in Children, Iowa City, Iowa, June 4-7, 1998.
16. Hodges, AV, Dolan-Ash, M, Balkany, TJ, Schloffman, JJ, Butts, SL. *Speech perception results in children with cochlear implants: contributing factors.* Otolaryngology Head and Neck Surgery 1999; 121:31-4.
17. Cullington, H, Hodges, AV, Butts, SL, Dolan-Ash, S, Balkany, TJ, *Comparison of language ability in children with cochlear implants placed in oral and total communication educational settings.* Proceedings of Seventh Symposium on Cochlear Implants in Children, Iowa City, Iowa, June 4-7, 1998.
18. Geers, A, Brenner, C, Nicholas, J, Uchanski, R, Tye-Murray, N, Rehabilitation factors contributing to implant benefit in children, Annals of Otology, Rhinology, and Laryngology, in press.
19. Schwartz, S, ed., Choices in Deafness, Bethesda, MD, Woodbine House, Inc., 1996.
20. Rhoades, EA, *Language progress with an auditory-verbal approach for young children with hearing loss,* International Pediatrics, 2001; 16:1-7.

COMMUNICATING WITH DEAF CHILDREN

AUDITORY-VERBAL (A-V) REFERENCES

Estabrooks, WM, ed., *50 FAQ's About AVT*, Toronto, Learning to Listen Foundation, 2001.

Estabrooks, WM, Schwartz, R, *The ABC's of AVT: Analyzing Auditory-Verbal Therapy*, Washington, DC, Alexander Graham Bell Association for the Deaf, 1995.

Estabrooks, WM, *A-V Therapy for Parents and Professionals*, Washington, DC, AG Bell Association for the Deaf, 1994.

Estabrooks, Warren, ed., *Cochlear Implants for Kids*, Washington, DC, Alexander Graham Bell Association for the Deaf, 1998.

Estabrooks, WM, Marlowe, J, *The Baby Is Listening*, Washington, DC, AG Bell Association for the Deaf, 2000. (Videotape)

Goldberg, DM, Flexer, C, *Outcome Survey of Auditory-Verbal Graduates: Study of Clinical Efficacy*, J Am Acad Audiol 4: 189-200 (1993).

Parents and Families of Natural Communication, Inc., *We CAN Hear and Speak! The Power of Auditory-Verbal Communication for Children Who Are Deaf or Hard of Hearing*, Washington, DC, Alexander Graham Bell Association for the Deaf, 1998.

Parents and Families of Natural Communication, Inc., *I Can Hear – I*, ('92), *I Can Hear – II*, ('96) AG Bell Assoc. for the Deaf, (Video)

Pollack, D, Goldberg, DM, Caleffe-Schenck N,, *Educational Audiology for the Limited-Hearing Infant and Preschooler: An Auditory-Verbal Program,* Charles C Thomas Pub Ltd; 1997.

Rhoades, EA, Chisolm, TH, *Global language progress with an auditory-verbal approach for children who are deaf or hard of hearing*, The Volta Review, 2001; 102:5-24. (Vol. 102, #1)

Tucker BP, *Cochlear Implants: A Handbook*, Chapter "*The Auditory-Verbal Approach: The Voices of Experience*," pp. 93-146, Jefferson, NC, McFarland & Company, 1998.

Vaughan, Pat, ed., *Learning to Listen*, Don Mills, Ontario, General Publishing Co. Limited, 1981.

Voice for Hearing-Impaired Children and Alexander Graham Bell Association for the Deaf, *Do You Hear That?*, 1992.

Wray, D, Flexer, D, Vaccaro, V, *Classroom performance of children who are hearing impaired and who learned spoken comm. through the A-V approach*, The Volta Review, 1997; 99:5-24. (Vol. 99, # 2)

[Contributed by Melissa Chaikof]

CHAPTER THREE

LANGUAGE DEVELOPMENT IN DEAF CHILDREN

by Frank Bowe, Ph.D., LL.D.

[Dr. Bowe is a professor and the special education coordinator at Hofstra University. He has played a role in virtually all major disability-related legislation enacted by the U.S. Congress. This includes the Individuals with Disabilities Education Act (IDEA), the Americans with Disabilites Act (ADA), as well as numerous telecommunications, televison decoder, and rehabilitation legislation.]

The highest priority in research and practice in deaf education, I believe, is finding ways for parents and teachers to facilitate language learning, as distinguished from the current emphasis on teaching language. Research and practice priorities in deaf education, accordingly, should focus upon fundamental questions of how deaf children and youth can learn language. This theoretical and review article presents personal opinions and invites responses from the field.

As we near the tenth anniversary of the report of the Commission on Education of the Deaf (Bowe, 1988), I believe our foremost challenge is to accelerate language development among deaf children and youth. The Commission's report has led to some real progress overall in education of deaf children and youth (see, for example, Bowe, 1991 and Bowe, 1993). Nonetheless, we face stubborn problems.

COMMUNICATING WITH DEAF CHILDREN

The challenge of which I write here is not an issue that government can or should address. As I put it in my keynote address to the 57th Biennial Conference of the Convention of American Instructors of the Deaf (CAID) in Minneapolis (Bowe, 1995b):

> We've done about as much as we're likely to do on national policy, at least for the foreseeable future. No one, least of all me, is satisfied with the state-of-the-art in deaf education. Further gains, however, are going to have to come at other levels, most especially in the classroom. What happens there is, and should be, beyond the reach of national policy.

Accelerating language development was the subject of "COED 3," the third of 52 recommendations made by the Commission. That recommendation captured the Commission's frustration with the seemingly intractable problem of facilitating linguistic competence in deaf students. It is a widely shared frustration. The general nature of the problem is well understood. Surveys by the Center for Assessment and Demographic Studies at Gallaudet (e.g., Allen, 1994), as well as research stretching back decades (e.g., Stuckless & Birch, 1966; Vernon, 1967), have shown a depressing pattern: Deaf students struggle to reach third- or fourth-grade reading levels by age 13 or 14, when students with normal hearing achieve at least seventh- or eighth-grade levels. During the high-school years, deaf students tend to "plateau" at those levels, rather than to advance further (see the Commission's final report, Bowe, 1988, pp. 15-24, and Braden, 1994, and Paul & Quigley, 1994).

These persistent low levels of mastery of English are especially disturbing to me because they occur as we move ever deeper into the "Information Age" -- a time in which our society places a premium on acquiring, analyzing, reporting, and using information. Mastery of written English is often essential for such work. My father was able to get and keep a good job despite not having completed college. The students of today are not likely to secure well-paying jobs unless they have the education and the skills to understand and use information.

Were they to be equipped with such competencies, individuals who are deaf could enjoy almost limitless academic and vocational success by tapping today's technologies (Bowe, 1994). An ever-growing proportion of business and other communications takes place today via email and fax. My consulting work these days is conducted almost entirely through email, fax, and the Internet -- all of which are 100% (or nearly so) visual communication mediums. As a deaf person, I am an equal-opportunity participant in these communication modes. What has fascinated me over the past five years is how eagerly my hearing colleagues have embraced these technologies -- because they seek refuge from time-consuming "real-time" voice telephone calls. There is, however, a caveat to all this: Virtually all of these services and products present information via the written word. In order to take advantage of these technologies, I must (all of us must) possess strong reading and writing skills.

COED's recommendation was that research and practice priorities be placed on helping deaf children to acquire language. For me, this principally means finding ways to help deaf children and youth to learn language. Notice that I did not say "to teach language to deaf children and youth." It is my personal opinion that linguistic competence is not at bottom something that can be taught; rather, it must be learned. The concept that our brains are wired to extract structure from innumerable sentences, whether heard or seen, and from them to generate a personal syntax, is both long-standing and well established (Chomsky, 1965). What it is not is well applied, in programs serving deaf children. To stretch the point somewhat, our brains do not take well to pedagogical presentations of the Fitzgerald Key (Fitzgerald, 1929). Yet the approach of teaching language, albeit no longer with the Fitzgerald Key, continues to this day to dominate education for deaf children.

Lest I be misunderstood here, let me emphasize that I am not saying that teachers of the deaf are not doing the best jobs they know how to do. I think by and large they are. Rather, they have not been given the tools to do better. Our task, as a field, is to develop, test, revise, and use such tools.

CURRENT APPROACHES

What I have seen in programs serving deaf children and youth, with few exceptions, are approaches that emphasize *teaching* language. These techniques are somewhat different from those the Commission reviewed in preparing COED 3. A good summary of the state-of-the-art at that time was offered by King (1984). She presented findings from a survey of 233 programs serving deaf children and youth:

> It can be seen that hearing-impaired children are frequently taught to produce, analyze, and correct sentences using some type of symbol system....Most programs (81.1%) also teach young hearing-impaired students to categorize words or sentences according to the categories of the symbol system. (p. 315)

King reported use of a variety of teaching strategies. Nonetheless, she acknowledges: "[N]o evidence supports any methods as the best approach for teaching language . . ." (King, 1984, p. 315).

More recently, some schools and programs have adopted whole language and bilingual/bicultural approaches. Whole language techniques -- despite the surface appeal of their call for "natural language" and to "teach language in context" -- are controversial in the reading field as a whole. In deaf education, I would expect them to be even more problematic: Whole language instruction assumes a fundamental mastery of the language by the student who is learning to read and write -- a mastery most deaf children clearly lack. In the past few years, particularly in center schools, we have also seen bilingual/bicultural approaches in which American Sign Language (ASL) is used as the primary language of instruction. Again, however, this seems to be occurring without the benefit of a careful examination of fundamental issues. The real danger in both techniques is that we may fail again, not because the approaches were not useful, but, rather, because we do not know how best to implement them (Fischgrund, 1997).

Through whatever techniques, schools and programs continue to attempt to *teach* language, rather than support its *learning* by deaf students. If I am correct that language must be *learned,* rather than *taught,* this immediately raises a question that King did not attempt to answer: How can teachers and parents facilitate such learning? I believe this is the central research and practice question in deaf education today.

SOME TOOLS

We do have some clues as to what we might do. My own experience, and that of other deaf adults with whom I have discussed this, such as Robert Davila and the late Terrence J. O'Rourke, is that reading during childhood -- a great deal of reading -- is what did it for us. In my case, I literally had no option. I had been "dumped" into a local school system which had never before worked with a deaf student; the unsurprising consequence for me was that time spent in class was not productive in advancing my education. And nothing on television was captioned. My only means to entertain myself were playing sports -- and reading. By the time I entered ninth grade, I had done so much reading that I had mirrored the linguistic input hearing children acquire without conscious effort. The result was the same for me as it was for them: from the innumerable instances of English, my brain had constructed a workable syntax -- and I had learned the language.

Today, television captioning offers another input mode that we should explore, especially with young deaf children. Many children's television programs, such as *Sesame Street* and *Mister Rogers' Neighborhood*, are captioned. The Telecommunications Act of 1996 (P.L. 104-104) requires that virtually all video programming be captioned by some time after 2001. Given television's strong appeal to children, captioning is a technology that offers real promise for accelerating language acquisition precisely because it provides the rich input that most children acquire via hearing and that I got from reading.

That, however, begs an important research question: How can deaf children, especially young ones, acquire language through, among other means, television and video captioning? Cartoons and other children's programming have been captioned for many years -- yet I have not seen over that period an accompanying rise in language competency among deaf children. Why is it that we have not yet realized the promise of this technology? Certainly, one possibility is that captioned videos may not have been made available to deaf children who are mainstreamed in the public schools (Davila, 1997). Still, one would have expected television viewing at home during the preschool years, and especially on Saturday mornings, to yield discernible results. I am particularly disturbed that I have seen so little research on captioning (aside from the work of Loeterman, below) in the past ten to fifteen years. We urgently need research and development in this area.

A related concept, for me, is that learning language should be an *active* process. This idea -- that deaf children learn language better and faster when they are active participants in the process -- is solidly grounded in important research by Peter de Villiers, the Sophia and Austin Smith Professor of Psychology at Smith College (viz., de Villiers & Pomerantz, 1992; Hoffmeister, de Villiers, Engen, & Topol, 1997). De Villiers testified on language acquisition before the Commission on Education of the Deaf.

The Clarke School for the Deaf, whose president Dennis Gjerdingen, was a member of the Commission, offers a curriculum that provides an example of active learning (de Villiers, Buuck, Findlay & Shelton, 1994). Another example is offered by the Lexington School for the Deaf, in Queens (Cohen, 1997). Lexington recently revamped its preK-12 curriculum to feature a conceptual framework for active learning. The approach stresses development by students of cognitive foundations, attitudes, and problem-solving skills that enable them to learn -- in school and out. Assessment of student progress calls for the students to apply, rather than just report, information.

I have also been impressed by the potential of American Sign Language (ASL) to enhance linguistic competence in deaf children. Research reported in an earlier issue of this journal by Michael Strong and Philip Prinz (1997) suggests quite strongly that the long-known tendency of deaf students who have deaf parents to excel academically over deaf students who have hearing parents appears to be attributable, in large part, to the fact that the former group is fluent in at least one language. That is, expertise in ASL could facilitate acquisition of English. Again, this begs an urgent research question: How, in practical terms, can we make that happen in our schools (Fischgrund, 1997)?

Clearly, we need to develop curricula in which ASL use accelerates English language competency, especially in the preschool years. Given the brain's developmental patterns, acquisition of *some* language during the early childhood years is essential. When parents, early interventionists, and preschool teachers are fluent in ASL, the use of ASL in everyday communication as well as in instruction may well be indicated, since it is a highly visible language, readily accessible to young deaf children as long as vision is not seriously impaired. All of this remains more theoretical than practical at this point. Fundamental questions remain unanswered: In day-to-day terms, what does the teacher do to use ASL to accelerate English language acquisition?

Even assuming answers to that question, some caveats remain about bilingual/bicultural approaches (Bowe, 1992). Because the vast majority of young deaf children have hearing parents, we cannot anticipate that ASL will be a first language for more than 10% to 15% of young deaf children. Although there are exceptions, my experience continues to be that most hearing parents cling to interventions based upon speech and lipreading, and resist learning ASL. Not many become fluent enough in the language to provide intelligible input for their young children. It may be time for us as a field to give up the long-held hope that all, or at least most, parents will master

ASL (Davila, 1997). Meanwhile, few early-intervention or preschool programs have children for more than a few hours each week (Bowe, 1995a); even if the teachers are highly skilled in ASL, they just do not spend enough time with the children to make up for the parents' deficiencies in the language. The potential of ASL for accelerating English language acquisition by young deaf children may therefore be much more limited than advocates of bilingual/bicultural techniques seem willing to concede.

In addition, I have another concern. Some advocates of using ASL with young deaf children insist also on delaying the introduction of English, including reading, until the later elementary school years (Moores, Walworth, & O'Rourke, 1992). I strongly oppose such notions, for three reasons. First, there is no reason to believe that exposure to more than one language limits the acquisition of any one language (see, for example, Strong & Prinz [1997]). Second, the brain's plasticity is such that if reading competence is not acquired by the mid-elementary years, children may never become comfortable with reading and writing. And third, as I mentioned earlier, my own experience and that of other deaf adults have been that reading is a linchpin to later academic and vocational success.

Looking at the middle-school and high-school years, I believe our greatest challenge is to assist deaf students to surmount the "plateau" that seems to stop continued progress. With these children and with adolescents, personal captioning shows considerable potential. Research in Boston by the WGBH National Center for Accessible Media and by the Center for Applied Special Technology suggests that deaf children and youth can improve their linguistic competence by captioning video programming (Loeterman, Kelly, Morse, Murphy, Rubin, Parasnis, & Samar, 1995). In this work, Mardi

Loeterman and her colleagues have shown that the opportunity to generate narrative captions to describe student-produced videos is highly motivating for deaf students, so much so that they persist in the effort until their captions efficiently and effectively describe the video.

As Loeterman's work suggests, there is a place for teaching of language. Even experienced writers need editors (I am no exception). Clear communication is a skill that must be honed over a period of years, and it is one that is greatly improved by expert review. For such editing to be effective, however, the writer needs to have already developed and internalized a coherent model of the language. That is why "teaching" language is something I believe is better suited to the middle- and high-school levels, as a supplement to active learning. For the preschool and elementary levels, I suspect the emphasis must be on supporting the "learning" of language rather than on its teaching.

That having been said, Loeterman's work supports the continuation with middle- and high-school age students of active involvement rather than passive absorption of knowledge. For the students who were captioning their own videos, language was a means to accomplish something; it had a social context that the students valued. It was not merely a memory requirement imposed upon them by adults. However, the question must be asked: Would the novelty quickly wear off? That is, is "personal captioning" helpful only on a short-term basis? We need longitudinal studies of the effectiveness of such approaches (Davila, 1997).

CONCLUSIONS

Our greatest need, it seems to me, is to research, develop, field test, and place into use a curriculum for parents and early interventionists to follow to give young deaf children an active learning opportunity in which they acquire mastery of language in all its forms. I see roles in such a curriculum for reading, for captioning, and for ASL. As Lexington's experience illustrates, changing to a curriculum that fosters active learning is not simply and quickly accomplished; it requires a program-wide and years-long commitment to staff training in order for it to become effective. That is, I think, a price worth paying; we must move away from the artificial teaching of language, simply because, from all available evidence, it has not worked.

Almost as important, I believe, is discovering ways to help middle- and high-school deaf students to surmount the "plateau" at which they seem to become stuck. I have been impressed by the work of Loeterman in offering active, highly motivating learning opportunities. This approach offers incentives for students to identify their own mistakes and to improve the clarity with which they express their thoughts. Although the specific technique of "personal captioning" may be useful only for a limited time, the general strategy of making linguistic competency meaningful strikes me as being precisely what adolescents and young adults need to continue their journeys toward linguistic competence.

The author thanks Oscar P. Cohen of the Lexington School for the Deaf, Robert R. Davila of the National Technical Institute for the Deaf, Joseph E. Fischgrund of the Pennsylvania School for the Deaf, and Nancy B. Rarus of the National Association of the Deaf for their contributions to the preparation of this article.

REFERENCES

Allen, T.E. (1994). Who are the deaf and hard-of-hearing students leaving high school and entering postsecondary education? Unpublished manuscript, Washington, DC: Gallaudet University Center for Assessment and Demographic Studies.

Bowe, F. (1991) *Approaching equality.* Silver Spring, MD: T.J. Publishers.

Bowe, F. (1995a). *Birth to five: Early childhood special education.* Albany, NY: Delmar Publishers.

Bowe, F. (1993). Getting there: Update on recommendations by the Commission on Education of the Deaf. *American Annals of the Deaf, 138,* 304-308.

Bowe, F. (1995b). Keynote address. Paper presented at the 57th Biennial Convention of American Instructors of the Deaf, Minneapolis, MN, June 25.

Bowe, F. (1992). Radicalism v. reason. In Moores, D. F., Walworth, M., & O'Rourke, T.J. (Eds.). *A Free Hand.* Silver Spring, MD: T.J. Publishers Inc.

Bowe, F. (1994). Technologies that hear and talk. *Technology and Disability,* 3, 1-10.

Bowe, F. (Ed.) (1988). *Toward equality: Education of the deaf.* Washington, DC: U.S. Government Printing Office.

Braden, J.P. (1994). *Deafness, deprivation, and IQ.* New York: Plenum Press.

Chomsky, N. (1965). *Aspects of a theory of syntax.* Cambridge, MA: MIT Press.

Cohen, O.P. (1997). Personal communication, May 13.

deVilliers, P.A., Buuck, M., Findlay, L., & Shelton, J. (1994). *A language arts curriculum for deaf students.* Northampton, MA: Clarke School for the Deaf.

Fitzgerald, E. (1929). *Straight language for the deaf.* Staunton, VA: McClure Company.

Hoffmeister, R.J., deVilliers, P.A., Engen, E., & Topol, D. (1997). English reading achievement and ASL skills in deaf students. *Proceedings of the 21st Annual Boston University Conference on Language Development.* Somerville, MA: Cascadilla Press.

King, C.M. (1984). National survey of language methods used with hearing-impaired students in the United States. *American Annals of the Deaf,* 129, 311-316.

Loeterman, M., Kelly, R.R., Morse, A.B., Murphy, C., Rubin, A., Parasnis, I., & Samar, V. (1995). *Students as captioners: Approaches to writing and language development.* Paper presented at the 57th Biennial Convention of American Instructors of the Deaf, Minneapolis, MN, June 27.

Moores, D.F., Walworth, M., & O'Rourke, T.J. (Eds.) (1992). *A free hand.* Silver Spring, MD: T.J. Publishers, Inc.

Paul, P.V., & Quigley, S.P. (1994). *Language and deafness.* (2e). San Diego, CA: Singular Publishing Group.

Strong, M., & Prinz, P.M. (1997). A study of the relationship between American Sign Language and English literacy. *Journal of Deaf Studies and Deaf Education,* 2, 37-46.

Stuckless, E.R., & Birch, J. (1966). The influence of early manual communication on the linguistic development of deaf children. *American Annals of the Deaf,* 106, 436-480.

Vernon, M. (1967). Relationship of language to the thinking process. *Archives of General Psychiatry,* 16, 325-333.

[Originally published in "Deaf Studies and Deaf Education," vol. 3, no. 1, Winter 1998, pp.73-78. Reprinted with permission from Frank Bowe, PhD.]

CHAPTER FOUR

COMMUNICATION MODALITIES AND ENGLISH LITERACY

by Gerilee Gustason, PhD.

[Dr. Gustason was deafened by meningitis at age five and attended public schools in Neb. and Calif. She received a B.A. in English from UC-Riverside, earned three master's degrees (in Education of the Deaf from Gallaudet U., in English from the U. of MD, and in Admin. and Supervision from San Fernando Valley St. C., now Calif. St. U., Northridge) and a doctorate in Educational Psychology from USC. She has taught at the Virginia Sch. for the Deaf, in mainstream classes in So. Calif., and at Gallaudet (teaching English and Education, and for a time chaired the Dept. of Ed). She is the co-developer of Signing Exact English and has given presentations in the U.S. and abroad. Most recently she headed the program preparing teachers of deaf and HOH students at San Jose St. U. She has served as the first deaf woman president of the Convention of American Instructors of the Deaf and on the board of the Council of Ed. of the Deaf, and as a grant reviewer for the U.S. Dept. of Ed. She is the mother of an adopted deaf teenage daughter.]

I am bemused at times by the furor over American Sign Language (ASL). Make no mistake, if I were not so involved with Signing Exact English, I would most likely be militant for ASL, because clear and comfortable communication for deaf kids is very dear to my heart. But it is hard for me to understand why some individuals tend to treat ASL as the ONE true religion and ignore what research truly does show us about communication and deaf kids. True, one's language is a very emotional topic of discussion. But if we really want clear information we should take an unbiased look at that research. What does it really say about ASL? What do we mean when we say ASL? PSE? SEE?

We could insist all we like that the sun comes up in the west, but unless we can find a way to reverse the compass, this does not make it so. We can insist all we like that ASL leads to improved English literacy, but unless research supports this concept this does not make it so.

To me ASL has long meant signs for concepts that are different from English words, put together in a grammatical order different from English. This is the whole basis for the argument for the acceptance of ASL as a foreign language in schools and colleges. We all know it can be difficult for an adult to learn a new foreign language, and learning ASL is no exception for most hearing people. As a result we often see PSE -- Pidgin Signed English, or the signs of ASL in English word order. But because PSE is just that, a pidgin, it does not represent either English vocabulary or English grammar. It was for that reason that SEE was developed -- to represent in signs what was spoken in English, and to add the grammatical markers such as –ing, -s, un-, etc. to truly show English on the hands.

I am labeled the "SEE lady" because I was one of the co-developers, and so I am. But it is important, I think, for educators and parents to understand what SEE is and is not. It is not a claim that everyone who purports to sign in English does a good job of it. (Neither, in point of fact, does everyone who claims to sign in ASL.) There are many individuals "out there" who sign poorly and read signs even less well. This is not the fault of ASL, or of SEE, but of the training (or lack of it) received by these individuals, and the evaluation and supervision (or lack of it) they have had. SEE is not an outright rejection of ASL. Many basic signs are common to both -- e.g. girl, know, want, food, silly, and so on. SEE is not a magic panacea to the problems of education of deaf kids; we need teachers who know how to teach, parents who can parent effectively, university teacher preparation programs that focus on meeting the needs of the individual child rather than marketing one answer for every kid. SEE is a means of showing on the hands what the inconsistent, crazy language we call English does with words, prefixes, and suffixes. SEE is easier to learn than ASL for native English speakers because they already know the language. This is important since over 90% of the parents of deaf children are hearing, and only about 3% of deaf kids have two deaf parents. Admittedly, SEE is also more time consuming to deliver than ASL because it involves more signs for the same number of concepts.

That said, what does research say?

In the 1960s and 1970s, research indicated deaf kids of deaf parents outperformed deaf kids of hearing parents raised orally. Brill (1960) found these two groups were similar in psychosocial adjustment. Stuckless and Birch (1966) found they were not really different in intelligence, and Meadow (1968) found no real differences in speech and speechreading skills. But the kids with deaf parents had superior reading and writing abilities and seemed to have both language and academic superiority. (See, for instance, Meadow, 1968 & 1975; Stuckless and Birch, 1966; Quigley & Frisina, 1961; Stevensen, 1964.)

What needs to be pointed out with these studies is that very few hearing parents were using any type of signs at the time, and most of these deaf children of hearing parents were raised orally. In the late 1970s this began to change. Brasel and Quigley (1977), for instance, compared four groups of deaf children: one group with deaf parents signing ASL, one group with deaf parents signing in English word order (which they labeled Manually Coded English, or MCE), one group with hearing parents and who were oral but didn't work at it, and one group with hearing parents and who were oral and DID work at it. The highest scoring students were those with deaf parents signing in MCE. Babb (1979) followed up on this with a study of deaf students with hearing parents and found that if the parents used SEE at home, the students were equal to those in the Brasel and Quigley study whose deaf parents signed MCE.

Strong and Charlson (1987) said that signing and speaking together, as is done with SEE or MCE and often with PSE, was an impossible task. Often quoted is a study by Marmor and Petito which showed experienced teachers signing only 5 to 8% of their sentences completely. It should be noted that the experienced teachers in that study totaled only two individuals. But Hyde and Power (1991), Swisher and Thompson (1985), Savage, Savage and Potter (1987), and Mayer and Lowenbraun (1990) also studied teachers and found that signing what was said could be as high as 98% complete if the teachers were properly trained and motivated. Moeller reported that parents could greatly increase the completeness of their signing when their awareness of what they were doing was increased and goals established.

This is important because, in the late 1980s, Moores and others (1987) found a strong relationship between correct English grammar usage and reading achievement. English-based signing for deaf kids with deaf parents correlated to writing ability, while only a low correlation was found between

ASL and reading or writing (Moores & Sweet, 1980). Luetke-Stahlman looked at deaf students from both deaf and hearing parents and found that students from families using spoken English, ASL, Seeing Essential English (SEE1), or Signing Exact English (SEE2) outperformed students exposed to Signed English or PSE (ASL signs in English word order). The students from families using SEE2 significantly outscored the others. Students from families using ASL outscored only the PSE students, and on only one of five tests. Similar high results for SEE students were reported by Moeller and Johnson (1988) and Schick and Moeller (1992). Moeller and Johnson documented ten years of reading and writing skills in a public school program using SEE and reported nine of twelve students were reading at or above grade level compared with hearing students.

Raffin, Davis, and Gilman (1978) studied deaf children using Signing Essential English, or SEE1, and found these students developing morphemic skills (the use of –ing, -s, etc.) in the same sequence as hearing children do. Looking at students who used Signing Exact English (or SEE2), Gustason (1981) used the Test of Syntactic Abilities (a test developed to evaluate the English skills of deaf students) and found young deaf students in programs using SEE outperforming the norming group of older deaf students. Gaustad (1986) found students with longer experience in signing English were similar to hearing students in scores and grammaticality, with marked improvement over time and the best results with children who started youngest. Schick and Moeller (1990) studied five SEE students in one program and found they used complex English structures similar to an older hearing control group. Luetke-Stahlman (1989, 1990) found that deaf students using ASL, spoken English, or SEE outperformed students using an incomplete representation of English such as Signed English or PSE, and that deaf students using SEE could understand deaf adults who used ASL.

This positive outcome is reported abroad as well. Schools in Singapore, for instance, use English. In 1977, most of the deaf students using either Shanghai Sign Language or spoken English failed the Primary School Language Examination (PSLE) required by the Ministry of Education. In 1978, the program began using SEE. The number of deaf students passing the PSLE has increased greatly since then. In 1983, out of 14 students, none received a credit pass on the O-level English results; in 1996, of 9 students, five passed. In 1983 only one deaf student was able to enroll in a junior college, while in 1997, 25 deaf students enrolled. The deaf adults there have expressed support of SEE. (Heng, 1998)

Such research has been largely ignored by individuals supporting the BiBi (bilingual/bicultural) approach, which advocates the use of ASL and the use of English only in reading and writing. This means students are taught English only in one class period a day, while instruction in every other subject (math, history, science, driver education, whatever) is conducted in ASL. We know from research with hearing students that time on task is a vital component of successful learning, and it is hard to understand how fluency in English can be obtained with such limited use of it. Research has not yet shown it can be done. Concerns on the lack of research supporting this BiBi model have been discussed by Moores (1992), Akamatsu and Fischer (1991), Marschark (1993), Mayer and Wells (1996), Menzel (1997), Newton (1985), Paul (1996, 1998a, 1998b), Paul and Jackson (1993), Paul and Quigley (1994), Rinne (1995), and Stuckless (1991).

This BiBi use of ASL has been advocated for over 20 years. (Cicourel & Boese, 1972a, 1972b; Johnson, 1989; Paul, 1987, 1990, 1991; Quigley & Paul, 1984; Reagan, 1985; Stokoe, 1975.) But none have conducted solid research showing this approach would work. The argument is simply that ASL is the native or natural language of deaf children. Advocates of ASL have assumed that if children develop high skills in ASL, which has no written form, they will be able to develop literacy in a second language -- English. Andrews, Ferguson, Roberts, and Hodges (1997) looked at seven deaf children between 4 and 7 years of age who had been taught with ASL, but deaf norms were used to measure achievement, which can be very misleading. Deaf children with "average" reading scores when compared to other deaf children are several years behind hearing peers. In addition, the two children with the highest reading scores had attended oral preschools not using signs, wore hearing aids, and preferred to speak. It is hard to understand how this data supports the BiBi model.

There are several noteworthy examples of programs using the BiBi model: the California School for the Deaf at Fremont, the Indiana School for the Deaf, and the Learning Center for Deaf Children in Framingham, Massachusetts. None of these have conducted research truly documenting age-appropriate literacy abilities in their students.

In 1997, Padden and Ramsey reported on a study comparing the students in the California School for the Deaf at Fremont with students in self-contained public school classrooms. (Note that this does not mention deaf students who are mainstreamed in public school classes with hearing students.) They reported that the public school students were more likely to have an additional disability, while the proportion of deaf students with deaf parents was five times higher in the residential setting. The study found no significant difference in reading at the elementary level, but the residential students outperformed the public school students at the middle school level. However, when the students with deaf parents were removed from the data, there was no significant difference between the two settings. Strong and Prinz (1997) also studied students at CSDF, and found a correlation between ASL skills and English skills, but used no reading measure and gave no comparison to hearing norms. Grushkin (1998) used outdated research to document that deaf students are visual learners and superior spellers, and promoted a whole-language approach and translation of ASL into English to improve deaf children's writing. In contrast, Paul (1998) reviewed the research literature on the whole-language approach and contrastive analysis and found none showing the effectiveness of these approaches.

What does all this show? If we look at research results, we can state several facts:

- Many individuals do not sign fluently, in either SEE or ASL.
- Teachers and parents CAN sign SEE with a very high degree of accuracy if trained and motivated.
- Deaf students exposed to SEE can understand adults using ASL.
- Deaf students exposed to SEE from a young age can develop complex English skills.
- Very little research exists on the use of ASL in developing English literacy, and this research is incomplete.
- The vast majority of parents of deaf children are hearing, and ASL is a language they would need to learn as a foreign language as adults. Fluency would be highly problematic under that condition.

- Most teachers, even those supposedly trained in ASL, end up signing PSE, which is neither English nor ASL and, research indicates, is the least effective communication method of developing English skills in students.

Finally, we should note that hearing aids are improving all the time, and more and more students are receiving cochlear implants. The use of ASL is not compatible with speech. Where does this leave the students who can benefit from hearing aids or who receive implants?

For some individuals, specifically deaf children with college-educated deaf parents, ASL/PSE may work fine. Their parents should have the right to make that choice. For others, cochlear implants work beautifully. Some may choose an oral route, or some form of assisted speechreading. For others, SEE may be chosen. ONE SIZE DOES NOT FIT ALL. We owe it to deaf children, and to their educational success, to look at what research tells us, at each child's needs, at each family's situation.

So far research has not told us that ASL leads to literacy, and it has told us that deaf children with hearing parents who use SEE can develop excellent English skills. Nothing works with every child, and nothing works alone. Good parenting, good teaching, high expectations, and good self-esteem are as important as clear communication.

REFERENCES:

Akamatsu, T., & Fischer, S. (1991) Using immediate recall to assess language proficiency in deaf students. *Am. Annals/Deaf,* 136, 428-434.

Andrews, J., Ferguson, C., Roberts, S. & Hodges, P. (1997) What's up, Billy Jo? Deaf children and bilingual-bicultural instruction in East-Central Texas. *American Annals of the Deaf,* 142 (1), 16-25.

Babb R. (1979) A study of the academic achievement and language acquisition levels of deaf children of hearing parents in an educational environment using Signing Exact English as the primary mode of manual communication. Doctoral dissertation, U. of Illinois.

Brasel, K., & Quigley, S. (1997) The influence of certain language and communication environments in early childhood on the development of language in deaf individuals. *Journal of Speech and Hearing Research,* 20: 95-107.

Brill, R. (1960) A study of adjustment of three groups of deaf children. *Exceptional Children,* 26: 464-466.

Circourel. A. V., & Boese, R. J. (1972a) Sign language acquisition and the teaching of deaf children: Part I. *Am. Annals/Deaf,* 117(1): 27-33.

Cicourel & Boese (1972b) Sign language acquisition and the teaching of deaf children: Part I. *Am. Annals of the Deaf,* 117(3): 403-411.

Gaustad, M. G. (1986) Longitudinal effects of manual English instruction on deaf children's morphological skills. *Applied Psycholinguistics* 7:101-128.

Grushkin, D. (1998) Why shouldn't Sam read? Toward a new paradigm for literacy and the deaf. *Journ. of Deaf Studies/D. Ed.,* 3(3):179-204.

Gustason, G. (1981) Does Signing Exact English work? *Teaching English to the Deaf,* Winter 1981.

Heng, C. L. (1998) An overview of 20-year development of total communication approach with Signing Exact English in Singapore (1977-1997). *Signal.* Singapore: The Singapore Assoc. of the Deaf.

Hyde, M., & Power, D. (1991) Teachers' use of simultaneous communication: Effects on the signed and spoken components.

Johnson, R., Liddell, S., & Erting, C. (1989) *Unlocking the curriculum: Principles for achieving access in deaf ed.* Gallaudet Research Inst. Occasional Paper Series, 89-3. Washington, D.C.: GRI, Gallaudet U.

Luetke-Stahlman, B. (1989) Documenting syntactically and semantically incomplete bimodal input to deaf subjects. *American Annals of the Deaf,* 133 (3):230-234.

Luetke-Stahlman, B (1990) Can SEE-2 children understand ASL-using adults? *American Annals of the Deaf,* 135(1): 7-8.

Luetke-Stahlman, B., & Moeller, M. P. (1990) Enhancing parent's use of SEE-II: Progress and retention. *Am. Annals/Deaf,* 135(5), 371-378.

Marmor, G., & Petito, L. Simultaneous comm. in the classroom: How well is English grammar represented? *Sign Lang. Studies,* 23: 99-136.

Marschark, M. (1993) *Psychological development of deaf children.* New York: Oxford University Press

Mayer, P., & Lowenbraun, S. (1990) TC use among elementary teachers of hearing-impaired children. *Am. Annals of the Deaf,* 135 (3): 257-263.

Mayer, C., & Wells, G. (1996) Can the linguistic interdependence theory support a Bilingual-Bicultural model of literacy education for deaf students? *Journal of Deaf Studies and Deaf Education* (2): 93-106.

Meadow, K. (1968) Early manual comm. in relation to the deaf child's intellectual, social, and communicative functioning. *American Annals of the Deaf,* 113: 29-41.

Meadow, K. (1975) A developmental perspective on the use of manual communication with deaf children. Paper presented at "Methods of Communication Currently Used Within the Education of Deaf Children" conference. See also Meadow, K (1980). *Deafness and child development.* Berkeley: University of California Press.

Menzel, O. (1997) Proficiency in ASL is not an alternative to literacy. *Deaf Life,* 28-30.

Moeller, M., & Johnson, D. (1988) Longitudinal performance of deaf students using manually coded English. Paper presented at ASHA National Convention, Boston.

Moores, D., Kluwin, T., Johnson, R., Edwoldt, C., Cox, P. Blennerhassett, L., Kelly, L., Sweet, C., & Fields, L. (1987) Factors predictive of literacy in deaf adolescents with deaf parents: Factors predictive of literacy in deaf adolescents in T.C. Programs. (Proj. # NIH-NINCDS-83-19, Final Rept.) Wash., D.C.: Dept. of Health and Social Services.

Moores, D. (1992) 1 hand clapping (editorial). *Am. An/Deaf,* 137 (4): 307.

Moores, D., & Sweet, C. (1990) Factors predictive of school achievement. In D. Moores & K. Meadow-Orlans (Eds.), *Educational and developmental aspects of deafness* (pp. 154-201). Washington, D.C.: Gallaudet University Press.

Newton, L. (1985) Linguistic environment of the deaf child: A focus on teachers' use of nonliteral language [English]. *Journal of Speech and Hearing Research,* 28: 336-344.

Padden, C., & Ramsey, C. (1997) *Deaf students as readers and writers: A mixed-mode research project.* Final report to the U.S. Department of Education. ERIC report ED413 688. San Diego, CA: U. of Calif.

Paul, P., & Gustason, G. (1991) Hearing impaired students'comprehension of high frequency multi-meaning words. *Remedial and Special Education (RASE)* 12 (4): 52-62.

Paul, P. (1996) First- and second-language English literacy. *The Volta Review* 98(2): 5-16.

Paul, P. (1998a) *Literacy and deafness: the development of reading, writing, and literate thought.* Boston: Allyn & Bacon.

Paul, P. (1998b) A perspective on the special issue of literacy. *Journal of deaf studies and deaf education,* 3(3): 258-263.

Paul, P., & Jackson, D. (1993) *Toward a psychology of deafness; Theoretical and empirical perspectives.* Boston: Allyn & Bacon.

Quigley, S., & Paul, P. (1994) *Language and deafness (2nd edition).* San Diego: Singular.

Raffin, M., Davis, J., & Gilman, L. (1978) Comprehension of inflectional morphemes by deaf children exposed to a visual English sign system. *Journal of speech and hearing research,* 21: 387-400.

Reagan, T. (1995) Neither easy to understand nor pleasing to see: The development of manual sign codes as language planning activity. *Language problems and language planning,* 19(2): 135-150.

Rinne, M. (1995) *Value and use of American Sign Language and English in two Pennsylvania schools for the deaf.* Unpublished doctoral dissertation, University of Pittsburgh, Pittsburgh, PA.

Schick, B., & Moeller, M. (1992) What is learnable in manually coded English sign systems? *Applied Psycholinguistics* 14: 313-340.

Stevensen, E. (1964) A study of the educational achievement of deaf children of deaf parents. *California News,* 80: 143.

Strong, M., & Charlson (1987) Simultaneous comm: are teachers attempting an impossible task? *Am. Annals/Deaf* 132, 376-382.

Strong, M. & Prinz, P. (1997) A study of the relationship between ASL and English literacy. *Journal of deaf studies and deaf ed.* 2(1): 37-43.

Stuckless, R. (1991) Reflections on bilingual, bicultural education for deaf children: Some concerns about current advocacy and trends. *American Annals of the Deaf* 136: 3.

Stuckless, R., & Birch, J. (1966) The influence of early manual communication on the linguistic development of deaf children. *American Annals of the Deaf,* 111: 452-460 and 499-504.

Swisher & Thompson (1985) Mothers learning simultaneous communication. *American Annals of the Deaf* 130, 212-217.

[This essay was contributed by Gerilee Gustason, PhD.]

CHAPTER FIVE

WHAT IS DEAF CULTURE?

A SOCIO-ANTHROPOLOGICAL PERSPECTIVE OF AMERICAN DEAF EDUCATION

by Patrick Seamans

[Patrick Seamans was born profoundly deaf, and his first language is French. He has a masters degree in Teaching English as a Second Language, and he was a National Leadership Fellow for TESOL International. He is currently completing his PhD in International and Intercultural Education at the University of Southern California.]

During the past decades, the deaf in the United States, as well as those in other countries, have been trying to define themselves within society. They constitute, indeed, a "different" population group, insofar as they are "disabled," and they also have their own language that they utilize for interpersonal communication. So, as a group, they are called "a group of disabled individuals," "a distinct Deaf Culture," "a linguistic minority," "a society," "a community," "a sub-culture," etc.

Then, which designation to accept, knowing that the "labeling" of a group refers to their social status, as well as to their needs for education? If this population group constitutes a "culture," they may require a "bilingual/bicultural" type of education. On the other hand, if the group is "disabled," special education may be more appropriate. It is essential to determine the true status of this population group, and whether or not the terminology refers to a completely homogeneous group (which is actually not the case) in reality. This is a necessary condition, prior to implementing educational methods, in order for the deaf to effectively access primary, secondary, and higher education.

THE SITUATION PRIOR TO 1973

With few exceptions, the hearing world, consciously or not, has indeed ignored the needs of the deaf, so much so that the feelings of isolation, of being separate and different, have had a great impact on the state of deaf children. In the past, the hearing world generally felt that the deaf were "deficient," "disabled," and unable to function equally to hearing persons in society.[1]

When laws were promulgated shortly after the Civil War making education compulsory for all, one of the underlying motives was to establish English firmly as the majority language, in an attempt to unify the diverse cultures existing in the United States and to make the country a "melting pot." The Union therefore survived, but at the cost of a serious degradation of many cultural traditions, including that of the Native American (American Indian) sign languages, and of the gestural language of signs of the deaf (much of which was first developed in France and then exported to the United States). These languages were viewed as "foreign languages," and it was felt that deaf persons had to be "restored" to the society of English speakers.[2] The educational system for the deaf focused on speech development and oral communication, generally resulting in failure and frustration for deaf children,[3] especially since the best lipreaders can only accurately understand about 20% of what is spoken to them.

COMMUNICATING WITH DEAF CHILDREN

Enrolled in a local school, a deaf child could only have a negative self-image of himself, as a result of his often difficult communicative relationships with teachers, staff, and other students.[4] In most of the United States, the deaf students were then placed in residential schools where they followed a special educational program, but which reinforced their segregation from general society.

In the residential school, the deaf child faced strict discipline, was limited in educational opportunities to the vocational level, and utilized American Sign Language (ASL) instead of the English language. He was encouraged to feel a sense of "belonging" to a "community," as well as to have strong fidelity to his school, his school peers, and to the gestural sign language in use at the school. In fact, people can identify the residential school attended by the ASL "accents" used by such persons. Sometimes, deaf teachers unintentionally passed on their bitterness towards the hearing world, and their own perception of their own limitations to their students, including their own lack of knowledge of the English language. As a result, the students acquired a limited, often skewed perception of the "outside" (hearing) world and of their ability to carve out a place for themselves in that world.

Thus, this pressure of belonging and complying, shared with other deaf persons, became a major theme in special education and formed the notion of a "deaf community," even though 95% of deaf children are born to hearing parents, the majority of whom do not know ASL. In these residential schools, deaf children are in frequent contact with older deaf persons, who have often lived through traumatic situations with hearing people, who never became fluent in English, and who prefer to avoid the general hearing society, giving up the benefits that exchanges with this society could have brought to them. As a result, deaf children develop a “learned inferiority complex,” which is reinforced by the fact that these schools have extremely poor reputations in academic education. It was shown, in a series of studies in the 1960s, that these children generally had a more negative self-concept as compared to other children.

THE SITUATION AFTER 1973

In 1973, the United States Congress enacted two laws: the Education of All Handicapped Children Act and The Rehabilitation Act of 1973. From then on, deaf students had the right to an “Individualized Education Plan” (IEP) to provide them with wide educational options, as well as the free provision of an English-based sign language interpreter (“Signed English” or “Total Communication” interpreter) in regular classrooms. Slowly, oralism and speech therapy became less important, while the goal for an appropriate education, based on the practice of sign language, modified to conform to the English language and used in regular classrooms, became paramount. This change in focus increased the chances of college-preparatory educational success for deaf students, who had previously feared attendance in regular classrooms.

As a result of this evolution toward acceptance of deaf students in public schools in the United States, more hearing parents enrolled their children in mainstreamed school programs. As a result, enrollment at residential schools dropped, and residential programs began to be shut down in many states. But, even though deaf teachers had the right, by law, to teach hearing students by using interpreters, school districts, in practice, were still unwilling to permit them to do so. As for the deaf administrators of residential schools, they did not stand a chance of obtaining new positions in local school districts.

And, even if some of these schools would have opened their doors to deaf teachers and administrators, these teachers and administrators continued to support residential schools. They appealed to the loyalties of their alumni and to the "deaf community" at large, to assist them in convincing the hearing world that contact between deaf students and deaf adults was an essential psychological requirement. Since it has been proved that deaf children born to deaf parents have higher self-esteem than those born to hearing parents, adaptation, in their minds, meant plunging all these children into the "deaf world" of residential schools. In addition, it was asserted that schooling with interpreters in regular schools did not meet the need for socialization of deaf students "with their own kind of people." Due to this popular and political pressure by the residential school advocates in many parts of the United States, the fallacy that "deaf taught by deaf is better education" gained support, and the residential school programs were retained.

Of course, logically, it is to be realized that the only reason that deaf children of deaf parents had more self-confidence than others was that the hearing parents of deaf children formerly tended to reflect stereotypical opinions regarding the potential of their children, which encouraged them to choose an oral education. Changing the opinions of the parents and having them learn effective methods for communication with their children could, and did, result in improved self-esteem for those deaf children. To this were added other benefits:

(1) The children, welcomed into the "hearing world," could succeed in the world and no longer be rejected. They had effective access to, and participated in, the majority culture.

(2) They received a general education that prepared them for postsecondary studies and were no longer restricted to the vocational programs of the traditional residential schools.

(3) Living at home with their parents, they could make friends with local children, both deaf and hearing.

(4) By combining hearing and deaf students, educators could innovate. For example, in Southern California, a new private elementary school for deaf children opened, named Tripod, which accepts hearing students who know gestural sign language, some of whom have deaf parents.

In higher education, since English-based sign language interpreters were also mandated by law, students started to enroll in often prestigious local and national universities and colleges, instead of the three traditional major "deaf programs": Gallaudet University in Washington, DC, National Technical Institute for the Deaf in Rochester, NY, and the National Center on Deafness at California State University, Northridge. Enrollment in these three programs has been decreasing.

A threat to the residential "special education of the deaf" at all levels, and to the employment of deaf teachers and administrators, was therefore perceived. In response, an idea was asserted by these deaf teachers and administrators, for the first time, that there was a "Deaf Culture" and that the only way to preserve that "culture" was to retain segregated residential schooling.

IS THERE A "DEAF CULTURE"?

In recent decades, there has been a movement within the deaf "community" to claim a definition for itself as a "separate cultural and linguistic minority group," even though this group previously properly recognized itself as a group of "disabled" persons. Thus, the focus has shifted from the field of sociology to that of anthropology.

Why did this change occur? The standard explanation is that the deaf "community" began to see itself differently because the use of the ASL gestural sign language created a "cultural system" instead of being merely an attempt to communicate English visually.

"Language is a cultural system" was stated in 1965 by Dr. William Stokoe, a professor of English literature, first known for "discovering" ASL at Gallaudet College (now Gallaudet University), then the world's only college completely accessible to the deaf. In the early 1960s, Stokoe began to apply Trager's linguistic principles to ASL. He relied on the fact that persons who use ASL "behaved differently" than those who used Signed English or Total Communication. The "Linguistic-Ethnographic Model of Deaf Culture" was the basis for Stokoe's research, and he expanded it into a new and distinct anthropological theory. Thus, this became the first indication of "Deaf (with a capital "D") Culture."

After Stokoe, the history of the "Deaf Culture" movement attracted more and more researchers, speaking about fields in which they often had no expertise, and using terminology that they do not always justify. G. Hans Furth, an empirical psychologist, stated in the Foreword to his book, *Thinking Without Language: Psychological Implications of Deafness:*

> "While I conducted and described my work as an empirical psychologist concerned with the thinking of deaf people, I realize that I have ventured into areas that are the proper concern of philosophy, education, anthropology, linguistics, hearing and speech, and rehabilitation. I may appear to have delved too deeply or too superficially into areas depending on the specialized knowledge of the reader, but I have tried to say nothing that is not

> scientifically defensible. My concern is primarily with the vital psychological reality of human thinking. *In this pursuit I did not hesitate to break with historically conditioned scientific approaches* that provide an inadequate conceptual environment for the questions and indeed the facts of the present investigations."[5]

Following this "breakthrough," other researchers began to wonder whether the "thinking processes" and behaviors of deaf persons were truly different than those of hearing persons, based on the fact that the gestural "natural" language of ASL has a different grammatical and syntactical structure than English. Finally, it was observed and noted that "deaf people do think like hearing people.[6]

But the movement toward ASL, of accepting a language that creates a separate culture, has continued until the present time, citing Stokoe's research as the basis for such assertion. The movement became stronger through the years, until today the term "culturally Deaf" is used to designate all of those persons (including hearing persons) who depend on, or utilize, ASL for their primary communication needs, and for whom the term "Deaf" is used in a capitalized form.

Thus, the trend that actually prevails in the United States, as well as in other countries now due to American influence, is marked by the formation of two separate groups of deaf persons: those who are simply deaf (who live in general society and use English), and those who are "culturally Deaf" (who follow the dogma of separatism and use of ASL that is strongly supported by the professionals from residential schools and activist researchers).

THE "CULTURAL" IMPACT ON EDUCATION OF THE DEAF

Since 1973, English-based sign language interpreters have been provided for deaf students in regular classrooms, and, in some cases, ASL interpreters have been provided. But, at the same time, the supporters of "Deaf culture" have influenced the continuation of the segregated school programs. The controversy has raged on. Should deaf children be educated within the "mainstream" cultural system, using standard grammatical English and participating in hearing classrooms with English-based interpreters? Or should they be considered a separate "cultural" group, in which deaf teachers and administrators, and segregated school environments using only ASL, are necessary?

In 1974, Lawrence Fleischer, deaf administrator of the Deaf Studies program at California State University, Northridge, analyzed "Deaf culture" according to the perspective of noted anthropologist Edward Hall: "Culture is communication and communication is culture." Fleischer then concluded that there were more differences than similarities between "Deaf culture" and the general mainstream culture in America, especially considering the special needs of the deaf population for unique modes of communication and social interaction.

Following this theme, now in vogue in the deaf community, it is asserted that deafness creates a separate "culture," but that its values would be destroyed by any effort to merge deaf children into the "hearing culture." From this perspective, "appropriate education" involves living with other deaf people for communication and social purposes. If this communication and socialization cannot be achieved, if the child is not exposed to "good" language and dialogue in ASL (thus implying that the use of English is "bad"), then one can expect a linguistic, intellectual, emotional, and cultural incomprehension in this child, unless it is imposed upon, to a larger or smaller degree, among the born deaf. "Most deaf children," Schein remarks, "grow up like strangers in their own households." However, this position does not now apply to hearing households deciding to learn one of the various modes of English-based sign language, or other modes of communication, such as Cued Speech, to communicate with the deaf members of their families; and this also does not apply to mainstream programs that now include English-based sign language, Cued Speech, and/or deaf teachers.

A DESCRIPTION OF "DEAF CULTURE"

Carol Padden, a hearing-impaired linguist, was the first to propose the model of "Deaf culture" in 1980, which then became the main argument in the deaf community for supporting residential, segregated education. According to Padden, the model of "Deaf culture" is valid at the anthropological level due to four "values" that create its originality:

a) There is a separate and distinct language (different from spoken languages) -- ASL.

b) Communication through speech and listening is not used.

c) The way of thinking, forms of socialization and behaviors are different from those of other cultural groups.

d) The stories of success and failure, the "folk tales," and other traditions are very different from those of the majority culture.

However, one can restructure all of these as follows:

1) This separate language of ASL is a simple communication system, developed by deaf people who did not master standard

English, and who needed a fast mode of communication; hence this is a type of purely gestural "short-talk."

2) There is no reason to use voice communication in the deaf community, since its participants cannot hear.

3) This "cultural group" behaves differently because of lack of information in gestural sign language as to "appropriate" behaviors. The socialization is different simply due to the fact of deliberate, forced segregation from hearing society by "Deaf Culture" advocates. And, it is definitely the knowledge level of the language, not the culture, that shapes the thinking styles of the deaf.

4) The individual stories of successes and failures and the "folk stories" are not the result of a cultural difference but of the exclusion of the deaf from general society; the deaf did not therefore master the ability to access the majority communications or culture.

In 1982, at Gallaudet University, Joshua Fishman gave a lecture on the social aspects of deafness, praising the borrowing of concepts and hypotheses from the social sciences to describe the socialization of the deaf child. But, at the same time, he warned about the limitations of metaphors and the risks of mistranslation, notably regarding the notions of "culture" and "ethnic group." Despite this caution, Simon Carmel, a deaf anthropologist, reinforced Padden's ethnographic model with frequent allusions to Keesing's cultural framework: "Cultures are epistemologically in the same realm as language." Accordingly, "language was the first part of the culture to be recognized."[9]

In actuality, language seems to be the one and only basis for considering deaf people to be a "culture," which is not enough to prove that a culture exists, according to standard anthropological criteria. Despite this, in the early 1980s, the University of California, Berkeley, Linguistics Department created a "Deaf Community and Culture" course. Other campuses followed this example, creating new employment opportunities for deaf teachers, who taught Deaf culture and introductory ASL courses.

The "Symbolic Model of Deaf Culture" was created in 1988, with a new book published by Carol Padden and Tom Humphries, *Deaf America: Voices from a Culture.*[10] Their rationale was based on the cultural anthropological thesis developed by Clifford Geertz, in which "culture" is defined as shared symbolic codes and meaning in social life. "[Culture] denotes an historically transmitted pattern of meanings embodied in symbols . . . by means of which men communicate, perpetuate, and develop their knowledge about and attitudes towards life. In contrast to the long history of writings that treat deaf people as medical cases, or as people with "disabilities" who "compensate" for their deafness by using (gestural) sign language, we want to portray the lives they live, their art and performances, their everyday talk, their shared myths, and the lessons they teach one another."[12]

Thus, from a "Deaf culture" point of view, deafness is an affective commitment, referred to as "attitudinal deafness," which has absolutely no relationship to audiological deafness. However, anthropologists working on other cultures have not been lax in raising strong criticisms of the obvious lack of logic in this viewpoint.

In an attempt to make a theory of "Deaf culture" more scientific, Oliver Sacks, a neurologist who does not know any form of sign language, proposed in 1989 an ethnoscientific model of "brain structure."[13] He claimed that the use of ASL since infancy creates a different way of thinking and, thus, a different brain structure. Although the linguists never perceived ASL as creating a different thinking pattern embedded in the brain, the "neurological" approach of Oliver Sacks has been well publicized, thus producing more confusion instead of clarity.

The "cognitive anthropology" of culture, pioneered by Hall and Trager, concerns itself with relationships among language, culture, and cognition. Kathee Christensen, a specialist in communication disorders, called for a new focus on Deaf culture and cognitive development. But, according to others, "since knowledge, ideas and values will vary in different members of society, a cognitive model from psychology cannot be applied to a culture as a whole."[14]

In short, Padden's ethnographic model presumes that language is a model of culture, "logically" equating with the ethnoscientific and cognitive model, so that culture becomes a system of ideas or a system of knowledge and concepts. This model and the "symbolic model" are accepted by many authors interested in Deaf culture. But these models are "illusory conceptual abstractions inferred from observations of the very real phenomena of individuals interacting with one another and with their natural environments."[15]

CURRENT ISSUES IN THE EDUCATION OF THE DEAF

In 1990, the United States Congress enacted the Americans with Disabilities Act, mandating that sign language interpreters be provided in all public and most private businesses, including private schools. The way is now open, more than ever, for deaf students to access the very best educational institutions in the United States, a conditional prerequisite to obtaining high-level employment based solely on merit and ability.

There is also now a nationwide relay service, provided free to deaf persons, along with free appropriate equipment for transmitted text (TTY/TDD in the United States, Minitel in France). Moreover, television programs are becoming accessible through closed captioning, along with a publicity campaign that highlights the potential for success of deaf persons. This logical governmental approach properly recognizes that the "deaf community" is a "minority group of disabled persons," which only needs facilitation of communication, and a bit more understanding, in order to become equal to hearing persons. The majority culture in America has recognized that deaf people have been unreasonably excluded, and is now trying to remediate that situation.

However, so as to preserve jobs and segregated programs nationwide, the movement in favor of "deaf culture" disagrees with the notion that the deaf can join with the majority culture. Harlan Lane, a hearing psychologist, asserts in *The Mask of Benevolence* that the deaf community "is not disabled" and that it is similar to the black and Hispanic communities as an ethnic/linguistic minority group that has experienced discrimination.[16]

In addition, Lane states, in his publications and in his lecture tours, the deaf community would rather have land provided by the government in order to run its own segregated society. But this is an extremist position by a hearing person, which very few "Deafcentrists" really support. Almost no one in the general deaf community would consider this option, now that there is increasing access to the majority culture and its benefits -- social, economic, and otherwise.

The most recent confusion was caused when it was asserted that "Deaf culture" is not limited only to deaf people, but is comprised of all persons who fluently communicate in ASL -- hearing children of deaf parents, hearing professionals who work with the deaf community, hearing ASL sign language interpreters, etc. This definitely indicates that, while there may be a linguistic "ASL culture," the fact is that "Deaf culture" is not exclusively composed of people who are deaf. In fact, since classes in ASL are now widely available to the general public in the United States, as part of the effort to establish recognition of ASL as a "foreign language," it must be noted here that the majority of "culturally deaf" people who use ASL have absolutely no audiological deafness or significant hearing impairment!

The "Deaf culture" deaf participants accept the social and employment benefits of the Americans with Disabilities Act, the financial benefits of Social Security Disability programs, and Department of Rehabilitation financial and employment assistance, as a "group of disabled people," while also asserting at the same time that they are "not disabled" and that they are simply members of a cultural, ethnic minority group. This "cultural group" has also recently accepted the fact that hearing people use their cultural language of ASL, and that many of the cultural variants came from their family environments.

CONCLUSION

The educational question remains more confusing than ever. Special education? Bilingual/bicultural education? Multi-cultural education? Is it preferable to enroll deaf students in regular schools to follow a general program of studies? Or should all deaf students be placed in segregated, primarily vocational schools run by deaf teachers and deaf administrators? Should we place students into school programs based on their use of ASL, or based on test scores that demonstrate their true ability to succeed?

According to Larry G. Stewart, a deaf psychologist, "Deaf culture," even yet to be satisfactorily defined, was not "discovered," but was actually created for sociopolitical purposes linked with the deaf community and their education. "Hence it is much more reasonable and logical to take the position that deaf people do not represent a separate culture in the deeper sense, but rather are in the main group of citizens, drawn together by their common communication needs, life experiences, and preferences."[17]

The Americans with Disabilities Act has a major role to play in providing the deaf community with full choice and equal participation, with a new focus on merit, ability, and potential, both in the majority society and in education. Instead of a focus on differences and limitation, this is a time for a new, holistic, conceptual framework that will make it possible to readjust and reappraise formerly negative attitudes toward people with disabilities.

NOTES:

1. P.C. Higgins, *Outsiders in a Hearing World: A Sociology of Deafness,* Newbury Park, Calif., 1980.
2. H.W. Hoemann, *Introduction to American Sign Language,* Bowling Green, Ohio, 1990.
3. M. Vernon and J. Andrews, *The Psychology of Deafness. Understanding Deaf and Hard-of-Hearing People,* New York, 1990.
4. V. Janesick and D. Moores, "Ethnic and Cultural Considerations," in: D. Moores et al. (eds.), *Toward Effective Public School Programs for Deaf Students: Context, Processes, and Outcomes,* New York, 1992.
5. G.H. Furth, "Preface," in: idem, *Thinking without Language: Psychological Implication of Deafness,* New York, 1996. My italics.
6. Ibid. My italics.

7. Quoted in: O. Sacks, *Seeing Voices: A Journey into the World of the Deaf,* Berkeley, 1989.
8. R. H. Winthrop, *Dictionary of Concepts in Cultural Anthropology,* New York, 1991.
9. S.J. Carmel and L.F. Monaghan, "Studying Deaf Culture: An Introduction to Ethnographic Work in Deaf Communities," in: *Sign Language Studies,* 73 (1990), pp. 411-20.
10. C. Padden and T. Humphries, *Deaf in America: Voices from a Culture,* Cambridge, Mass., 1988.
11. C. Geertz, *The Interpretation of Cultures,* New York, 1973.
12. C. Padden and T. Humphries (note 10 above).
13. O. Sacks (note 7 above).
14. C. Seymour-Smith, *Macmillan Dict. of Anthropology,* London 1986.
15. M. Sahlins, *Culture and Practical Reason,* Chicago, 1976.
16. H. Lane, *The Mask of Benevolence: Disabling the Deaf Community,* New York, 1992.
17. L. Stewart, "Debunking the Bilingual-Bicultural Snow Job in the American Deaf Community," in: M.D. Garretson (ed.), *Eyes, Hands, Voices,* National Association of the Deaf, 1996.

[This essay previously appeared in Diogenes Vol. 44/3 (1996), Reprinted with permission from Patrick Seamans and Poala Costa Giovangigli, Editor.]

CHAPTER SIX

CUED SPEECH AFTER 30 YEARS: A COMPILATION OF INTER-NATIONAL RESEARCH RESULTS

by Paulette R. Caswell, JD, PhD.

[Paulette Caswell has both a MS and PhD in International and Intercultural Education from the University of Southern California. She holds a MS in Bilingual Education in addition to the JD. She also holds a number of bachelor degrees in most other major areas of study. Dr. Caswell is focused on the pursuit of logic and rationality through scientific research and the avoidance of pseudoscience.]

Cued Speech (CS), more descriptively known as "Cued Speechreading" (CS-reading), is a system of using hand cues with lipreading to make spoken languages completely visually accessible. The system was invented in the 1960s at Gallaudet University by Dr. R. Orin Cornett, initially for use with hearing impaired individuals, but the system has now been determined to be of benefit to speakers of second languages, persons with normal hearing in learning phonetics and lipreading, and those with learning disabilities (apraxia, dyslexia, etc.). The CS system is not a "separate language," but is based simply on the phonological representations of spoken language. CS can be learned in only *18 hours,* with fluency and normal speech speed attained after a short period of practice.

After 30 years of use, CS is used worldwide, and it is now the law in France that all hearing impaired students be taught in this system, as it has proved to result in native fluency of spoken language, resulting in literacy abilities for even the most profoundly deaf students who became deaf prelingually, at a level equal to, or even exceeding, the literacy levels of their hearing peers. At this time, the CS system has been adapted for use in all of the major languages of the world. It is time to compile the research results by category, in order to provide an essential guide for administrators and educators wishing to utilize CS in their own educational programs.

PEDAGOGICAL ISSUES

English Language

1996: "Interview: R. Orin Cornett, Ph.D., Father of CS," Bonillas, Paula, Hearing Health, 12, 26, 2.

1995: "Exeprience des Parents," Le Couster, B. & V., LPC Info. No. 89, March, 1995, 405.

1994: Guidelines and Policies: National CS Association, CS Journal, V, 65-80. *Outlines guidelines and policies for the production and approval of CS materials, terminology guidelines for use in material, and guidelines on the mechanics of cueing.*

1994: "A Parent Planned Camp for Families and Professionals," Balderson, L., Paper presented at the AG Bell Conv, Roch., NY, 1 July '94.

1993: "NCSA Terminology Guidelines for CS Materials," Cornett, R.O., NCSA-USA Autumn, 1993.

1992: The CS Resource Book for Parents of Deaf Children, Cornett, R.O. & Daisey, M., NCSA-USA, 1992 (ISBN 0-9633164-0-0)

1987: "Progress and Perspectives: 1987," Cornett, R.O., CS Annual, 3, 1-16. *Fascinating account by the inventor of the CS system of the process of development, and the utilization of the system in schools, worldwide, during its first 2 decades of use, with recommendations for the future.*

1987: "Cuereading Skills Development," Turner, A.M., CS Annual, 3,45-48. *Outlines the process of developing skills in cuereading, identification of some problem areas, and some minor criticisms.*

1987: "Don't Just Talk, Say Something! Generalization of Speech Targets Into Everyday Language Use," Sneed, N., CS Annual (Apdx. - Paper presented at the first annual Conf. of the CS Assoc.), 3, 78-79. *Guidelines for teachers and parents in using games and other techniques during the "Carryover" phase of speech development (the process of actually using the learned production of sounds in everyday speech).*

1986: "Teaching With CS: The Middle Years," Lee, B., CS Annual, 2, 3-21. *Outlines teaching methodologies for CS programs in the first school system in Louisiana to recognize CS as an intervention tool. Goals and objectives are stated for a five-year language program.*

1986: "The Self Monitoring Cue Card Format: What It Is and How to Use It," Jones, C., CS Annual, 2, 62-66. *Outlines a code used to record spoken and cued information, using two written codes, Foneemik Spelling and cue notations, and the use of cards and the CS system in the classroom and in therapy sessions. Applications include therapy for persons having one or more of the following problems: hearing sensitivity loss, auditory perceptual confusion, reading disability, dialectal distortions, spelling difficulties, dysfluency in conjunction with misarticulations, and dyspraxia.*

1985: "What Can CS Do For You?," Beck, Pamela H., CS Annual, 1, 9-18. *Comprehensive summary of the benefits of CS, written for all professionals (including physicians, allied health professionals, audiologists, speech-language pathologists, teachers of the deaf, school administrators, educators in total communication programs, health education program planners, and hearing aid dealers); senior citizens centers; deafened adults and their families, friends, associates and employers; and families of hearing-impaired children.* ***Indications are that there are many other applications for CS, including use in foreign language instruction.***

1985: "Some Thoughts on Profitable Research Directions Regarding CS," Gregory, J., CS Annual, 1, 19-25. *Summary of research results, with recommendations for more concerted research efforts, and a call for a centralized database center on CS users.*

1985: "Breaking Through the Attention Barrier," Barwell, M., CS Annual, 1, 26-29. *Recommendations for getting very young children to pay attention to cueing.*

1985: "The CS Connection," Barwell, M., CS Annual, 1, 32-37. *History of the Nat'l Child Research Center and its CS program.*

1985: "A Test for CS Proficiency," Beaupre, W., CS Annual 1, 38-45. *Explanation of the standard testing method for assessing CS proficiency, now known as the BCSPR (Basic CS Proficiency Rating), which is required for certification as a CS Transliterator or Instructor. Add'l information contained in: 1986: "The CS-reading Test: An Analysis of the Results," Beaupre, W.J., CS Annual, 3, 32-40.*

PEDAGOGICAL ISSUES

Deaf Education

1995: "Queries Abound: CS -- An Update," Dixon-Millar, J., BATOD Association Magazine, January, 1995. *Includes discussion of other communication modes used in deaf education.*

1995: "Education Policy: The Views of Young People and Their Parents," Paper presented at the 18th International Congress on the Education of the Deaf (ICED), Tel Aviv, Israel, 20 July 1995.

1994: "Accelerating English Acquisition and Reading Development in Total Communication and Aural/Oral Programs," Cornett, R. O., CS Journal, V, 37-54. *Describes the role of parents and teachers in the utilization of CS with deaf children, and the use of the Auditory/ Visual model to increase skill development in audition. Recommendations on how CS can be integrated into Total Communication, Auditory/Verbal, aural/oral, and bilingual "natural signed language" programs. Shows how CS provides freedom from signed communication modes in teaching English.*

1994: "The Importance of Thinking Words," Cornett, R.O., CS Journal, V, 1-7. ***"Only if in face-to-face communication, as a result of that communication, a child consistently thinks English words, will that child learn English rapidly and efficiently. This is true whether the child has an auditory deficit or not."*** *Issues of forgetting, remembering, and the learning of English for deaf students in Total Communication and Aural/Oral programs are discussed.*

1994: "CS: What's the Big Deal?" Koo, D., Volta Voices, July/August 1, 1994, 1,4, 23.

1993: "Chapter 2: Manual Systems," Technology and Alternative and Argumentative Communication, College of Speech Language Therapy, London, 1993, 210-221.

1992: The CS Resource Book for Parents of Deaf Children, Cornett, R.O., & Daisey, M., NCSA-USA.

1987: "Cue to My Face, But Please Talk Behind My Back! Combining Unisensory Auditory Training and CS," Dowling, B., CS Annual, 3, 55-59. *Recommends that auditory training be continued during the process of deaf education using CS. Recommendations for early identification of deafness, fitting two hearing aids, giving full opportunity for the child to use residual hearing ability, and the use of CS for speech correction, clear communication in noisy environments, and more.*

1987: "Kindergarten: Fun or Frustration? Language-Based Criteria for Mainstreaming," Fletcher, P., CS Annual (Appendix - Paper presented at the first annual Conference of the CS Association), 3, 67-68. *Outlines criteria used for assessment of language-based curricula used in kindergarten, including the types of testing to be used, and three types of mainstreaming possibilities, as well as the criteria for deaf students remaining in mainstreamed classes.*

1986: "The Teaching of CS to Hearing-Impaired Adults," Turner, A.M., CS Annual, 2, 34-41. *Provides information on teaching CS to hard of hearing or deafened adults, with special problems noted, classroom hints, and other practical information.*

1985: "Mainstreaming: It Can Be More Blessed to Give Than to Receive," Efron, R., CS Annual, 1, 30-31. *Written in 1977, this is an account of the first deaf child to be mainstreamed with CS into regular courses with hearing children.*

1985: "Teacher-Pupil Interaction in Oral and CS Classes in England and Australia, Power, D.J., Int'l Congress on Education of the Deaf, Manchester, England. *This study evaluated the levels of teacher dominance. Results: Teacher dominance was highest in oral classes in England, next in oral classes in Australia, and much lower in CS classes in both England/Australia. There is a marked superiority for CS classes in pupil initiative and pupil initiation of communication.*

French Language

1994: "Que Sont Nos Enfants Devenus?" Boroy, A., ALPC-France, LPC Info. No. 84, August-September 1994, 4-6.

INTERNATIONAL EDUCATION

1994: "Adapting CS to Additional Languages," Cornett, R.O., CS Journal, V, 19-29. As of October, 1993, *CS had been adapted to 56 languages and major dialects. This paper describes the adaptation techniques, the basic theory of CS, the procedures followed in assigning phonemes to Cued procedures for adaptation to other languages and dialects in the future, timing CS movements, special problems, and the use of CS in dual-language households.*

1994: "The Use of CS in Learning Foreign Languages," Dixon-Millar, J., Presented at the 4th Conference of the European Fed. of Parents With Hearing-Imp. Children (FEPEDA), Southampton, 25-29 July 1994.

1994: "CS and Bilingualism," Jones, S., Paper presented at the 4th Conference of the European Federation of Parents With Hearing-Impaired Children (FEPEDA), Southampton, 25-29 July 1994.

1992: The CS Resource Book for Parents of Deaf Children, Cornett, R.O., & Daisey, M., NCSA-USA.

United States

1995: "Deaf Students Attending Regular Four-Year Colleges and Universities in the United States," Menchel, R.S., Paper and Thesis presented at the 18th International Congress on the Education of the Deaf (ICED), Tel Aviv, Israel, 10 July 1995.

1995: "Closing of CS Program (at Gallaudet University, Washington, DC) a Terrible Mistake," The Weiss Family, Silent News, March, 1995.

1994: "Toward Full Participation: Young Deaf Adults Speak Out," Hurowitz, A., Koo, D., McIntosh, R., & Scher, S., Paper presented at the A.G. Bell Convention, Rochester, NY, 30 June 1994. *Students from the National Technical Institute of the Deaf in Rochester, NY and the University of Maryland describe their use of CS.*

1993: "Benefits of Early Communication Through CS," CS Team, Gallaudet U, Washington, DC., Jan. 1993. Amended to English-English.

Great Britain

1996: "Our Experiences With CS in Great Britain and Europe," Jefferson, A., Unpub. paper presented at the AG Bell Con., Utah, July, '96.

1995: "The Development and Use of CS in the United Kingdom,1970-1995," Dixon-Millar, J., Paper presented at the 18th Int'l Congress on the Education of the Deaf (ICED), Tel Aviv, Israel, 19 July 1995.

1994: "A Brief Outline of the Involvement of The Nat'l Centre for CS in Kent and Canterbury," Dixon-Millar, J., Unpub. paper, July 1994.

1993: "Communication is Your Responsibility," Dixon-Millar, J., The Progress Report of the National Centre for CS to the Panel of Four. The Friends House, Euston Road, London, 25 May 1993.

1993: "Deafened People Can . . . Communicate," Dixon-Millar, J., Network, 32, Summer, 1993. *Summaries of the talks given at the meeting held at London House, 22 May 1993.*

1992: "CS: How It Helps Many Deafened Adults to Continue to Use and Understand Everyday Spoken Language at Home and Elsewhere, and So to Remain Integrated in Hearing Society," Dixon-Millar, J., Network, Autumn, 1992, 12-13.

1992: "LPC - CS en Grande-Bretagne: La Percee est Arrivee, "Dixon-Millar, J., Second European Congress on Langage Parle Complete, Brussels, 15 November 1992.

1987: "CS in Great Britain," Dixon-Millar, J., CS Annual, 1, 60-65. *CS was introduced in England in 1971, and this article outlines the activities of the Nat'l Ctr. for CS, which opened in Dec. 1975, and the use of CS in schools in England. Additional information is provided on the use of CS in N. Ireland, Scotland, and an effort to introduce the program in Wales; adult ed. programs in England; religious services; in mainstreamed activities with hearing students, and more.*

France / Belguim

1995: "Les Implants Au Quotidien: l"U. des Franche-Comte," Fed. Nat'l des Orthophonistes (FNO), LPC Info. No. 91, May 1995, 2-4.

1995: "Les Journees D'Etudes Chambery," ALPC-France, LPC Info. No. 90, April, 1995, 2-5.

1995: "Conditions de Reussite et Risques d'Echec Dans l'Utilization du LPC: Tentative d'Analyse," Charlier, B., Journees Nationales du LPC, Chambery, 1st April, 1995, 7.

1994: "Oralisme et Bilingualisme," Perier, O., ALPC-France, LPC Info. No. 85, October-November 1994, 5-6.

1987: "The Education of the Deaf-Current Perspectives, Vol. 1, 1985 International Congress on the Education of the Deaf," Perier, O., Charlier, B., Hage, C. & Alegria, J., CS Journal, 4, 1990. *This paper summarizes the reasons for the adoption (in 1980) of both CS and Signed French for teaching deaf students in the programs of the Centre Comprendre et Parler and the Ecole etegree, both in Brussels.* ***Results:*** *1.) There are wide differences in the benefits obtained from CS; 2.) Most children derived substantial benefit from CS, in the reception of spoken language; 3.) The use of CS at home is more beneficial than its use at school, and children who used CS both at home and at school performed best.*

1986: "Signs of Life: Proceedings of the Second European Congress on Sign Language Research (pp.194-199)," Perier, O., Bochner-Wuidar, A., Everarts, B., & Michiels, J., CS Journal, 4, 1990. *This paper describes the initial rationale, methodology, and results associated with the innovative experimental use of both manual communication and CS in a preschool program for deaf students.*

Spain

1995: "La Palabra Complementada en el Centro CREDAG Narcis Maso -- La Macana," Marin, C. & Peges, A., Fed. Espanola de Asoc. de Padres y Amigos de los Sordos, FiAPAS, No. 43, Mar.-Apr. 1995, 43-46.

1993: "En Tomo A Una Practica de Intervencion Visivo-Manual Con Ninos Sordos," Cedillo, P., Medina, P., & Seguin, J.L., Federacion Espanola de Asociaciones de Padres y Amigos de los Sordos, FiAPAS, No. 32, July-August 1993, 38-42.

1993: "PC, Lectura, Fonologia Y Sordera," Escolen, R., Federacion Espanola de Asociaciones de Padres y Amigos de los Sordos, FiAPAS, No. 32, May-June, 1993, 50-51.

1993: "Il Congreso Europeo de Palabra Complementada: Bruselas, los dias 14 y 15 de nov. 1992," Escolen, R., Fed. Espanola de Asoc. de Padres y Amigos de los Sordos, FiAPAS, No. 30, Jan-Feb. '93, 42-45.

Germany

1974: "CS im Vergleich zum Mund-Hand-System nach Forchhammer," Musmann, Roswitha Winker, Unpublished master's thesis, Padagogischen Hochschulke Rheinland, Abteilung fir Heilpsdogogik, Ksln. *CS was compared with a previous system developed in Denmark by G. Forchhamer in 1923, known as the Mund-Hand-System (M-H-S).* ***Results:*** *"In conclusion, CS, in comparison with M-H-S, is of greater effectiveness in relation to spoken language and for spoken communication, and the adaptation (of CS) to German is most highly desirable for use in spoken German."*

LANGUAGE ACQUISITION

English Language

1996: "CS, ASL and Multilingualism," Hurowitz, A., & Koo, D., Unpub. paper presented at the Nat'l Assoc.of the Deaf Conv., July, 1996.

1995: "Complete Signed, Cued and Spoken Language; A Means for Hearing Parents to Present Their Own Language in a Completely Acceptable Form to Their Own Deaf Children," Hage, C., & Perier, O., Paper presented at the 18th International Congress on the

Education of the Deaf (ICED), Tel Aviv, Israel, 20 July 1995.

1994: "The Importance of Thinking Words," Cornett, R.O., CS Journal, V, 1-7. *"Only if in face-to-face communication, as a result of that communication, a child consistently thinks English words, will that child learn English rapidly and efficiently. This is true whether the child has an auditory deficit or not." Issues of forgetting, remembering, and the learning of English for deaf students in Total Communication and Aural/Oral programs are discussed.*

1994: "Sound and Vision," Jefferson, A., Therapy Weekly, Macmillan, 17 November 1994, 6.

1992: "Can Both Auditory Listening and Language Acquisition Be First?" Cornett, R.O., & Dowling, Beth, Paper presented at the A.G. Bell Convention, San Diego, CA, 20 June 1992.

1990: "Receptive and Expressive Language Abilities of Hearing-Impaired Children Who Use CS," Berendt, H., Krupnik-Goldman, B., & Rupp, K., Unpublished master's thesis, Colorado State University, Fort Collins. *36 deaf CS subjects, aged 5-16 years old, were assessed to see if CS produces rapid learning of the English language.* ***Results:*** *Students averaged at the 92nd percentile of the hearing-impaired peers of the same age. CS children correctly produced an average of 36.5 sentences, a result comparable to that of hearing children.*

1987: "Language Development Through Communication With CS," Daisey, M.E., CS Annual, 3, 17-31. *A "down-to-earth" discussion about language and the impact of communication with CS. Implications for deafness, including the basics of language development, bilingualism, written language and reading, early education and the parents' role, and an outline of relevant research.*

1986: "CS as a Phonological Model," Beaupre, W., CS Annual, 2, 22-33. *Outlines the fact that CS is phonemic, not phonetic, and provides lingustic information about the CS system.*

French language

1989: "CS and Language Acquisition," Hage, C., Alegria, J., & Perier, O., CS Journal, 4, 1990. *9 prelingually deaf children were assessed as to their knowledge of gender-based nouns. 60 nouns were used, familiar and unfamiliar, masculine and feminine, and marked by endings and unmarked.* ***Results:*** *The deaf students scored 80% on the marked words, showing that they had absorbed the gender rules related to* *word endings. On familiar words, they scored 90% on unmarked, and close to 100% on the marked words.*

ENGLISH AS A SECOND LANGUAGE (ESL) EDUCATION

1994: "The Importance of Thinking Words," Cornett, R.O., CS Journal, V, 1-7. *"Only if in face-to-face communication, as a result of that communication, a child consistently thinks English words, will that child learn English rapidly and efficiently. This is true whether the child has an auditory deficit or not."*

1984: "The Effects of CS on the Auditory Discrimination of English Vowels by Hearing Chinese Speakers," Chapman, I.M., Unpub. master's thesis, U. of Miss. *4 Chinese adults, with 7-10 years experience in the English language and with normal hearing were taught CS, to measure the effects on discrimination of spoken vowel and dipthong sounds of English.* ***Results:*** *All vowels and dipthongs were correctly discriminated when both the visual mode of CS and the auditory mode were employed. With audition only, after CS, there were only two common errors in identification of vowel sounds, and none for diphthongs. All had improvement in the Aural Comprehension Test.*

PHONETICS AND LIPREADING

English Language

1996: "CS Brings Clarity to Lipreading," Dixon-Millar, J., Crosswords Magazine, Spring, 1996, ATLA, 38, 16, 3. 1975: "The Effects of Training in CS on Syllable Lipreading Scores of Normally Hearing Subjects," Sneed, N.A., CS Parent Training and Follow-up Program, 38-44. Project Report to U.S. Office of Ed, Dept. of Health, Ed. and Welfare, Washington, D.C. *10 normally-hearing college students, ages 18-23, were trained in phonetic notation, pretested, and then given 15 hours of CS instruction over a period of 6 weeks.* ***Results:*** *1.) Identification of phonemes rose from 11% to 14.9%, significant at the .01 level; 2.) Identification of consonants rose from 24.4% to 27.4%; 3.) Identification of vowel phonemes rose from 42% to 54%, also significant at the .01 level.*

1979: "Effects of CS on Lipreading Ability," Chilson, R.F., Unpublished master's thesis, U. of RI. (Also pub. as "Effects of CS Instr. on Speechreading Skills," CS An., 1, 60-68.) *Analysis of previous research invalidating that the trad. methods for instructing the deaf have not been effective in overcoming language limitations.16 nor-*

mal hearing college students were assessed against a control group to see if CS improved their lipreading abilities, all of whom were in the same course with identical phonetic and transcribing education. ***Results:*** *The group that learned CS had a significant improvement in their lipreading abilities, with significance at the .01 level.*

1977: "CS as a Training Strategy in Phonetics Courses," Beaupre, W.J., Int'l Assoc. of Logopedics/Phoniatrics Congress Proceedings, 2,35-41.

1976: "Effects of CS Instruction on the Mastery of Certain Phonetic Transcription Skills," Tate, M.B., Unpublished master's thesis, U. of Rhode Island. *48 normally-hearing college students were divided into two groups of 24 persons each, to provide control and experimental groups. The control group received traditional phonetic instruction in a classroom using workbooks, while the experimental group received independent CS instruction with an experimental workbook and materials.* ***Results:*** *The experimental group obtained higher scores than the control group, with differences significant at the .05 level.*

1974-75: "What is CS," Cornett, R.O., Gallaudet Today, 5:2, 28-30. *Review of research, including Sneed's study. Normal hearing college students were assessed before and after CS training on 348 nonsense syllables.* ***Results:*** *1.) Average scores increased from 75% to 95%; 2.) Average scores on uncued material increased from 11% to 14.9%.*

AUDITORY SOUND RECOGNITION

English Language

1991: Results of study carried out by teachers and parents of children who use CS, The CS Resource Book for Parents of Deaf Children, Cornett & Daisey, 1992. *11 deaf children were assessed in 1991, all of whom received CS instruction for several years in the home, on the ability to recognize 20 unfamiliar words in Spanish.* ***Results:*** *CS usage raised unisensory auditory identification scores by 74%, and aural/oral identification scores by 162%.*

1987: "CS and Audition: Partners or Rivals?," Richey, J., CS Annual, 3, 49-54. *Outlines the objections of "oralists" that CS visual movements distract attention from auditory input. Reviews previous studies, identifies the elements of speech processing, addresses the issues of individual differences, and concludes that more research is necessary.*

1987: "CS and the Role of Auditory Learning," Latt, J.M., CS Annual (Appendix - Paper presented at the first annual Conf. of the CS Assoc.), 3, 75. *CS and auditory learning in general are discussed.*

An integrated approach is proposed, and the role auditory learning plays in the overall development of speech skills and the reception of spoken language is discussed.

French Language

1986: "Speech Audiometry and CS," Charlier, B., & Paulissen, D., Otica, 10, 19. *9 prelingually and profoundly deaf subjects at 13 years old mean age were studied after 52 months of exposure to CS, to see if CS interfered with their use of residual hearing.* ***Results:*** *"The subjects of this research were effectively able to utilize the support of the cues to improve their auditory recognition. And, far from diverting the auditory attention of the children, the presence of the cues from CS was able to support in them a better phonetic discrimination through audition."*

Other Languages

1985: "The Effects of CS Upon Tonal Reception of the Thai Language by Hearing-Impaired Children," Tammasaeng, M.C., Dissertation Abstracts Int'l, 47(01) 150A. *36 profoundly deaf fifth-grade students in the Sethsatian School for the Deaf in Bangkok, ages 12-16, were assessed. 9 students were trained in speech with signs, 27 were using signs and fingerspelling only. Lipreading and CS were taught to all subjects for one semester.* ***Results:*** *1.) Tone perception for audition alone was 49.5% (chance=50%), while with cues it was 86.2%; 2.) The children from the speech class scored at 96.9%, while those trained in only signs and fingerspelling scored at 82.6%; 3.) On lipreading alone, both groups scored at chance. CS helped clarify the tonal characteristics of the Thai language for profoundly hearing-impaired Thai students, since the perception of the tonal characteristics is essential to an understanding of the Thai language.*

RECEPTIVE LANGUAGE SKILLS -- SPEECH RECEPTION

English Language

1995: "Phonological Representations in the Deaf: How Can This Competence Be Enhanced?" Hage, C., Paper presented at the 18th Int'l Congress on the Ed. of the Deaf (ICED), Tel Aviv, Israel,10 July 1995.

1994: "CS and the Ling Speech Model: Building Blocks for Intelligible Speech," Perigoe, C.B. & LeBlanc, B.M., CS Journal, V, 30-36. *"The goal of CS is to give the hearing-impaired child clear and precise spoken language input. The goal of the Ling speech method is to give the hearing-impaired child clear and intelligible spoken lang-*

uage output." Recommends an integrated approach using CS and the Ling system for speech production, describes general speech development issues, and outlines the use of the combined method in producing better voice patterns, vowels and diphthongs, blends, consonants, and carry-overs. Recommendations for use by teachers/parents.

1989: "CS and Language Acquisition," Hage, C., Alegria, J., & Perier, O., CS Journal, 4, 1990. *55 subjects were compared for improvement in reception of spoken language through CS.* ***Results:*** *Performance was highest when children received CS both at home and at school, somewhat lower for those who received CS only at home, and lowest for those who received CS only at school. Additional Results: 1.) Higher degrees of hearing loss result in less ability to speechread; 2.) Speechreading improved with the use of CS; 3.) Longer duration of exposure to CS, and starting CS at an early age, both result in improved levels of spoken language acquisition.*

1987: "Background Variables as Predictors of Cued Speechreading Proficiency," Gregory, J.F., CS Annual (Appendix - Paper presented at the first annual Conference of the CS Association), 3, 69-70. *Presentation centered around two related questions as to background variables, with a general linear model used.*

1987: "Response Patterns in a S-reading Task Involving CS," Gregory, J., CS Annual, 3, 41-44. *11 hearing impaired subjects, aged 11-68 were assessed. 5 had prelingual losses, the remainder postlingual losses. 2 were hard of hearing, while the remaining 9 were "deaf" but not severely enough to be categorized as profoundly deaf.* ***Results:*** *1.) Consonant identification with CS did not seem to differentiate between "easy" and "hard" words; 2.) CS may not offer much help with vowel-initial words.*

1985: "Discourse Comprehension by Hearing-Impaired Children Who Use CS," Musgrove, G.N., Doctoral dissertation, McGill U., Montreal. *20 profoundly deaf children between 10-18 years old, all with normally hearing parents, with least four years of using CS, were assessed as to ability to understand three types of story text: conversational, narrative, and explanatory.* ***Results:*** *1.) The deaf children were found to be more competent at understanding conversationally organized text than the other two types. With this type of text, the deaf students performed at the same level of reading-level-matched hearing children; 2.) The hearing students focused on the story's problem in the* *narrative form, while the hearing-impaired students focused on events leading up to the program and on dialogue; 3.) The deaf students' scores were similar to the reading-level-matched hearing children on the explanatory passage.*

1979: "CS and the Reception of Spoken Language," Nicholls, G., Unpublished master's thesis, McGill U., Montreal. *18 profoundly hearing-impaired subjects, who had used CS for at least four years, were assessed by speech-reception tests.* ***Results:*** *1.) Speech reception scores of over 95% with the key word in sentence materials, and over 80% with the syllables were obtained with lipreading plus cues, and audition plus lipreading plus cues; 2.) There were large individual differences in using audition only; 3.) Speech reception abilities were highly correlated with speech production, while language attainments were correlated with reception through CS.*

1975: "CS: An Evaluative Study," Ling, D., & Clarke, B., Am. Annals of the Deaf, 120, 480-488. *12 hearing-impaired subjects, age 7-11 were studied. These children had been exposed to CS one to two hours a day for one school year.* ***Results:*** *Scores were generally superior when material was presented with cues, but the students had not had enough exposure to CS (see follow-up study) to process the material in more than word units.*

1974: "The Effects of CS on the Speechreading Ability of the Deaf," Kaplan, H., Dissertation Abstracts Int'l, 36(2), 645B. *18 severely and profoundly deaf adolescents were evaluated as to language ability.* ***Results:*** *1.) CS significantly improved speechreading scores for all types of materials used; 2.) Improvement did not depend on IQ, receptive vocabulary, reading level, or lipreading ability; 3.) Improvement was significant for words and unrelated sentences, but not for related sentences; and 4.) There was some minor ambiguity in the cues used in a few consonant pairs.*

RECEPTIVE LANGUAGE SKILLS -- READING

1996: "CS Frees the Families and Cultivates Reading Skills," Caldwell, B., Rupert, J. & Elsie-Daisey, M., Unpublished paper presented at the A.G. Bell Convention, Utah, 28 July 1996.

1996: "CS: Facilitating Reading Acquisition for the H-I.," Knight, J., Unpub. paper presented at the AG Bell Convention, Utah, 28 Jul. '96.

1995: "Language Experience, Not Deafness, Determines the Acquisition of Reading and Spelling," Laybaert, J., Unpub. paper presented at the 18th Int'l Congress on the Ed. of the Deaf (ICED), Tel Aviv, Israel.

1994: "Why Johnny Can Read," Caldwell, B., CS Journal, V, 55-64. *Comprehensive paper on reading research. Outlines general research, models and theories in reading, general information about CS, research studies in general education reading, studies in reading with children who have developmental language disorders, and studies of skilled deaf readers. Research indicates that the use of CS is highly beneficial in producing skilled readers.*

1989: "Use of Internal Speech in Reading by Hearing and Hearing Impaired Students in Oral, Total Communication, and CS Programs," Wandel, Jean E., Unpublished doctoral dissertation, Teacher's College, Columbia U, NY. *120 hearing imp'd students were tested [(30 Oral, 30 TC, 30 CS, 15 from each group being profoundly deaf (90 dB loss or more in the better ear, and the other 15 being severely deaf (65-89 db loss in the better ear)], along with 30 hearing students as a control group. All students had no secondary disabilities, ability to read the stimuli words, and English as the primary language spoken at home, as well as a history of using the relevant communication mode for at least 3 years. Tests included the Raven Standard Progressive Matrices (RSPM), the 1982 SAT reading comprehension test, and the Conrad "Inner Speech" assessment.* ***Results:*** *1.) Overall, the hearing-impaired students had lower scores than the hearing controls; 2.) The CS and Oral groups scored significantly better than the TC students; 3.) The CS /Profoundly Deaf group and the hearing group achieved the same scores on the SAT reading comprehension test; 4.) The CS/Severely Deaf group had lower scores than the CS/ Profoundly Deaf group. Results indicate that the CS users possess reading strategies similar to those of hearing students, but which are different from those used by Oral and TC students.*

1986: "Reading Development in Hearing-Impaired Children," Cornett, R. O., CS Annual, 2, 42-61. *Provides information on the theories of reading; a special-purpose model of reading development for prelingually deaf children; a reading development model; general applications of the model; and the special applications of the model for children who use ASL, Pidgin Signed English, Manually Coded English, Fingerspelling, A/V, Auditory/Oral and CS prior training.*

COMMUNICATING WITH DEAF CHILDREN

French Language

1989: "Role Played by the CS in the Identification of Written Words Encountered for the First Time by Deaf Children," Alegria, J., DeJean, C., Capouillez, J.M., & Leybaert, J., CS Journal, 4, 1990. *18 children - 14 profoundly deaf, 4 with severe hearing loss, who had used CS for an average of 2 years, with research on the ability to understand new words.* ***Results:*** *"The lexicon developed by the deaf with CS has properties which are equivalent to the phonology of hearing subjects. In both cases, the internal representations of the words are compatible with their orthographic representations. This allows the use of phonological coding to identify unfamiliar words, and, as said before, can prime the whole process of reading acquisition."*

1988: "Role of CS in the Identification of Words in the Deaf Child: Theory and Preliminary Data," Alegria, J., Lechat, J., & Leybaert, J, CS Journal, 4, 1990. *16 deaf children - 14 profoundly deaf from birth, 2 severely deaf from birth, and a control group of 16 children with normal hearing, with research on the ability to understand words from context, and whether the deaf children used CS to develop the ability to identify nonsense words.* ***Results:*** *The deaf children utilized CS as an intermediary in the activity of reading, in a similar manner to methods used by the hearing children.*

1988: "CS and the Acquisition of Reading by Deaf Children," Leybaert, H., & Alegria, J., CS Journal, 4, 1990. *This paper delineates clearly and logically the rationale for the probable need of prelingually deaf children for access to the phonological code of the language they learn, in the process of acquiring it as a base for reading.* ***Results:*** *The conclusion is that CS might help to overcome the reading difficulties generally encountered by deaf subjects, since CS seems to enable the deaf children to develop addressed and assembled phonological codes.*

EXPRESSIVE LANGUAGE SKILLS

English Language

1994: "Development of Expressive Communication Skills With CS," Quenin, C., Nat'l Tech. Inst. of the Deaf, Rochester, NY. Paper presented at the A.G. Bell Conv., Rochester, NY, 30 June 1994.

1991: Data on language of profoundly deaf children with oral, signing and CS backgrounds. Unpublished data and analysis supplied by correspondence. Annotated in The CS Resource Book for Parents of Deaf

Children, Cornett & Daisey, 1992. *36 deaf children, 5-11 years old, with backgrounds in Signed English, oral training, and CS were assessed as to verbal language skill abilities.* ***Results:*** *The CS users scored 86%, 80%, and 71% on three tests used. In comparison, the Oral/Aural students scored 13%, 22%, and 11%, and the students taught in Signed English scored 17%, 10%, and 5%.*

1987: "A Comparison of the Intelligibility of Cued and Uncued Speech," Sheridan, M.C., CS Annual (Appendix - Paper presented at the first annual Conf. of the CS Assoc.), 3, 76-77. *6 hearing-impaired children who had been cueing for at least 3 years were assessed as to their abilities in speech, both with and without cues.* ***Results:*** *A significant improvement in speech intelligibility occurred when students cued while speaking.*

1976: "The Effects of Using CS: A Follow-Up Study," Clarke, B., & Ling, D., The Volta Review, 78, 23-34. *8 profoundly deaf 8-12 year old subjects, who had been tested the previous year for their ability to identify and write down sentences and phrases using CS, were again tested.* ***Results:*** *Scores were significantly superior to the previous year, when the material was presented with cues. Sentence accuracy rose 50.8% with cues, and 13.6% without cues. For word accuracy within sentences, a rise of 26.6% with cues, and 12.1% without cues.*

French Language

1994: "An Acoustic Study of the Speech Skills of Profoundly Hearing-Impaired Children Who Use CS," Ryalls, J., Auger, D., & Hage, C., CS Journal, V, 8-18. *30 children were studied (10 with normal hearing, 10 with profound hearing impairments who did not use CS, and 10 with profound hearing impairment who had used CS for at least five years).* ***Results:*** *CS provides somewhat better speech skills for hearing impaired children than for their hearing-impaired non-cueing peers. Results for the CS group were always between the normally-hearing group and the non-CS hearing-impaired group. CS users had better VOT distinctions for bilabials and alveo-dentals, shorter syllable durations and lower fundamental frequencies than their peers who did not use CS.*

1987: "The Psycholinguistic Integration of Signed French and CS: How Can Speech Components be Triggered?," Perier, O., CS Journal, 4, 1990. *1.) Anecdotal evidence shows that the use of both CS and Signed French by deaf children leads to psycholinguistic integration. 2.)*

The combination of CS and Signed French can support the development of expressive speech.

CASE STUDIES (1-3 Research Subjects)

English Language

1996: "My Experiences With CS," Plail, G., Crosswords Magazine, Spring, 1996, ATLA, 38, 19, 1.

1994: "See Hear: I Cue," Beck, P.H., Hearing Health, January, 1994.

1994: "Interpersonal Discourse: A Prelingually Deafened Child and Hearing Peer," Sneed, N., & Kretschmer, R.R., Paper presented at the A.G. Bell Convention, Rochester, NY, 30 June 1994.

1987: "Aural Habilitation Prior to Cochlear Implant of a Congenitally Deaf Child," Lasensky, J.A., & Danielson, P.M., CS Annual (Appendix - Paper presented at the first annual Conference of the CS Assc.), 3, 71-72. *Description of a five-year-old nonverbal deaf child, and the use of CS, which resulted in a rapid increase in acquisition of receptive language, improved lipreading skills, expanded vocabulary, greater ability to comprehend complex and abstract language, increased vocalizations, consistent visible articulatory movements, subvocalization in play, and an improved ability to sound out words on a phonetic basis. A vibrotactile aid was also utilized, resulting in improved speech capability.*

1987: "Case Study: CS Training for a Deaf-Blind Ten-Year- Old," Lasensky, M.S., & Danielson, P.M., CS Annual (Appendix - Paper presented at the first annual Conference of the CS Association), 3, 73-74. *Study of a 12-year-old girl with Usher's Syndrome, introduced to CS for two and a half years.* ***Results*** *showed significantly improved production of all vowels and most consonants. Vibrotactile aids were also used. Speech intelligibility significantly improved, but decreased when the cues were not present.*

1986: "Signs of Life: Proceedings of the Second European Congress on Sign Language Research (pp.194-199)," Perier, O., Bochner-Wuidar, A., Everarts, B., & Michiels, J., CS Journal, 4, 1990. *In one case study, a deaf boy's parents had to switch over gradually to almost total use of CS, because the boy's linguistic progress with CS quickly passed the level of language that could be signed by his parents.*

1986: "CS: A Miracle for Mark," Rehjon, M., & Barris Perigoe, C., CS Annual, 2, 67-74. *Description of language acquisition and training of a prelingually, profoundly deaf boy in Ottawa, Canada, prior to, and after utilization of the CS system. Includes testing results and spoken language samples.*

1985: "Analysis of an Oral Language Sample from a Prelingually Deaf Child's CS: A Case Study," Kipila, B., CS Annual, 1, 46-59. *Analysis of videotaped conversations by a prelingually, profoundly deaf child at age 5 years, 4 months. The child has unclear speech, and has used CS since age 2 1/2. In 111 utterances, the child produced 100% accuracy on seven morphemes: contractible auxiliary, past irregular, past regular, plural, possessive, third person irregular, and uncontractible copula. The articles were 90% correct, and the 4 not correct were omissions. Uncontractible copula was 80% correct and the child scored 2 out of 3 correct in uncontractible auxiliary and 3 out of 5 correct in present progressive. Of the 15 errors, 10 were omissions, 5 were errors of usage, and there were no overuse" errors.*

1984: "CS: A Single Case Study," Christopher, S., Unpublished master's thesis, Texas Woman's U., Denton. *Outlines one family's attempts to provide an education for their profoundly deaf daughter utilizing CS.*

1983: "The Effects of CS on the Language Development of Three Deaf Children," Mohay, H., Sign Language Studies, 38, 25-49.*The language development of three prelingually deaf children was studied monthly as the children learned CS, only to evaluate spoken language production.* ***Results:*** *With CS, 1.) The frequency of use of communicative gestures diminished dramatically; 2.) A slight shift toward the production of longer spoken utterances occurred.*

1973: "Cues or Signs: A Case Study in Language Acquisition," Nash, J. E., Sign Language Studies, 3, 80-91. *A case study of a single child concluded that the "normal language acquisition (of English) appear not to be present in the cues." Response by Dr. Cornett (same issue): The parents of this child did not have guidance on how to stimulate expressive cueing in that one child. The only other prelingually, profoundly deaf child (at that time) who had received CS consistently prior to age one, Janette, had a spontaneous spoken vocabulary of 210 words and phrases and a much larger receptive vocabulary by 22 1/2 months of age. Janette's father stated, "There is evidence to suggest that the use of CS with a very young child permits the maintenance of a normal sequence of development of speech and language despite the existence of a significant hearing impairment."*

1972: "A Study of the Readability of CS," Cornett, R.O., CS Parent Training and Follow-Up Prgm., 45-52. Project report to U.S. Office of Ed., Dept. of Health, Ed. and Welfare, Wash. DC. *1 profoundly deaf 15-year-old CS user was compared to an 8-year-old hearing CS user, to determine pure identification of speech sounds and words without any auditory input.* ***Results:*** *The deaf child correctly transcribed 96% of the syllables, with 98% accuracy on the phonemes in the syllables, and 90% of the words with 96% accuracy on the phonemes. Without cues, she scored 42% on syllables and 53% on words. The hearing child scored 88% on cued syllables and 96% on cued words. Without cues, she scored 27% on syllables and 13% on words. Listeners with normal hearing scored between 80% and 96% on a similar test.*

French Language

1995: "Le Langage Parle Complete Pour Integer Les Sourds: Jeremie, Etudiant, Comme Les Autres," ALPC-France, LPC Info. No. 88, February, 1995, 8.

1995: "Des Nouvelles de Stasie Jones," Jones, S., LPC Info. No. 91, May, 1995, 6-7.

1995: "CS et Bilinguisme par Stasie Jones," Jones, S., LPC Info. No. 94, October 1995, 2-4.

1978: "Le CS, un Complement Visible du Langage Parler," Juillerat, C. & Mantelet, E., Combined master's theses, Academie de Paris - Universite de Paris. *Detailed case studies of two profoundly deaf children, Stasie and Isabelle. Each provides information on background, family efforts, learning and use of CS, language development, speech and behavior. Notes from Dr. Cornett: Stasie was the first child in France to be exposed to CS. She was 16 years old in 1990, has attended only French schools, always mainstreamed, and without an interpreter. She is fluent in both spoken and written English and French, with excellent speech in both, has studied German for several years, and has also taken Russian in school.*

Spanish Language

1995: "Metodo de la Palabra Complementada: Experiencia Personal," Colomer, C., FiAPAS No. 47, November-December, 1995, 45-46.

1992: "La Palabra Complementada: Complementado Con Mi Hijo," Escolen, R., Federacion Espanola de Asociaciones de Padres y Amigos de los Sordos, FiAPAS, No. 28, September-October 1992, 53-55.

CUED SPEECH TRANSLITERATORS

1994: "Certification -- It's Not a Luxury," Koo, D., January, 1994.

1994: Guidelines and Policies: National CS Assoc., CS Journal, V, 65-80. *Outlines guidelines and policies for the production and approval of CS materials, terminology guidelines for use in material, and guidelines on the mechanics of cueing.*

1994: "CT & CSTs: The Risk of Carpal Tunnel Syndrome," NCSA-USA, CS News, Fall 1994.

1993: "Cueing the Word "Jumped," Cornett, R.O., 12 October 1993.

1993: "NCSA Terminology Guidelines for CS Materials," Cornett, R.O., NCSA-USA, Autumn, 1993.

1992: The CS Resource Book for Parents of Deaf Children, Cornett, R.O., & Daisey, M., NCSA-USA.

1987: "Cuereading Skills Development," Turner, A.M., CS Annual, 3, 45-48. *Outlines the process of developing skills in cuereading, identification of some problem areas, and some minor criticisms.*

1985: "A Test for CS Proficiency," Beaupre, W., CS Annual, 1, 38-45. *Explanation of the standard testing method for assessing CS proficiency, now known as the BCSPR (Basic CS Proficiency Rating), which is required for certification as a CS Transliterator or Instructor. Additional information contained in: 1986: "The CS-reading Test: An Analysis of the Results," Beaupre, W.J., CS Annual, 3, 32-40.*

OTHER RELEVANT ARTICLES

1996: "Dial 888: Subtitling for Deaf Children," Gregory, S., & Sancho-Aldridge, S., ITC Research, ISBN 0-900485560, Feb., 1996, p.46.

1995: "Les Implants Cochleaires, Response d L'APLC au Monde," ALPC-France, LPC Info. No. 87, January, 1995, 1-2.

1994: "Experience of Using Vibrotactile Aids with the Profoundly Deaf," Phillips, A.J., Miligan, J., Downie, A., Thornton, A.R.D., & Worsfold, S., European Journal of Disorders of Comm., 17-26 & 29.

1992: Abstract: "Analytic Study of the Tadoma Method: Improving Performance Through the Use of Suppl. Tactual Displays," Cornett, R., MIT, Journal of Speech & Hearing Research, 35, 450-465, Apr., '92.

(Compiled and contributed by Paulette Caswell, JD, PhD.)

CHAPTER SEVEN

ENGLISH ACQUISITION FOR DEAF CHILDREN
by Glenn T. Lloyd, Ed.D.

[Glenn T. Lloyd is a retired former teacher and administrator in schools/programs for deaf children and a Professor of Special Education after having taught at the University of Tennessee, New York University, and Lenoir-Rhyne College. He was elected Editor Emeritus and Lifetime Member of ADARA, having served nearly 20 years on its Board of Directors, including a term as President. He also served as Executive Secretary of the North Carolina Association of the Deaf, as Chair of the Board of Education for the NC Schools for the Deaf and Chair of the NC Rehabilitation Council.]

When I first began to work in the field of education for deaf children, I had no idea of what I was getting into. In the first place, I assumed that 13- and 14-year old boys and girls would be able to understand me since we would all be speaking English. I really had no practical concept of what being born deaf or becoming deaf early in life meant when it came to the knowledge and skills we normally hearing persons pretty much take for granted. Just by living, we acquire the ability to speak, understand, and use English. How naïve and wrong I was.

One of my primary tasks, as a teacher of deaf children, was to help them 'refine' their English composition skills. To do this, we were to use a device called the Fitzgerald Key.

Using the Fitzgerald Key, one could analyze a sentence and/or write a sentence in correct English. At least that was the theory. The Fitzgerald Key, in 1955, was a huge mystery to me and still is. It did remind me of the exercises we did in grade school, called diagramming sentences. It didn't help, though, because I never mastered the 'art' of diagramming either. In a word, it was a mystery to me to utilize the Fitzgerald Key to teach English to the children, and I was constantly seeking the help and guidance of the teacher in the classroom next to mine. Regardless, the children did no better in using English after a year with me than they were doing when I entered the classroom to teach them.

When I came back to the same school after a year at Gallaudet University earning a master's degree in Education for the Deaf, the same children were no better off in terms of being able to handle English than the year before. In fact, I noticed that most of the children in the school, whether older than my class or younger, failed in the ability to use English 'naturally' and 'normally'. I found the same condition in the Kendall School, the on-campus school for deaf children at Gallaudet, and it firmed up, for me, the realization I had arrived at during my first year, that deaf children simply don't learn English. Thus, 1955 was a year that brought me face-to-face with a problem that has intrigued me ever since.

In today's world, I don't see that there is any real improvement in the results of efforts by most residential schools for deaf children to instill English in their graduates. Most graduates, who were deaf from their earliest years, still are not demonstrating mastery of English. I can also attest from personal experience that many of the graduates from Gallaudet, at least through the early 1990s, similarly did not demonstrate mastery. A review of the history of education for deaf children shows that ever since the first state school for the deaf was established nearly 200 years ago, we have been endeavoring to teach English to deaf children. Basically, it seems we are no better at it today than we were back then.

In spite of the fact that some deaf children do succeed in learning English, I have reached the conclusion that it is less than useless to try to teach (formally teach) English to a majority of deaf children -- even as a second language. (When I speak of "formally teaching English," I refer to efforts at teaching English as a classroom exercise, much the same as many persons with normal hearing studied Latin, French, Spanish, or German during their high school years.) Those of us with normal hearing learned English long before we ever entered grade school. We learned it because it was the language used in our homes and neighborhoods. Formal English instruction came later.

American Sign Language (ASL) may well be an authentic language, but I am not aware that it has been codified. Every language, every legitimate formal language, has rules, etc., that help its users understand the proper construction of the language. After learning English during our pre-school years, we learned the rules of English all through our school years, including college. We didn't just acquire English, we were taught the rules of English. Knowing the rules of our primary language, I suspect, helps students go on to learn, formally, another language beginning in high school, most likely. "Knowing" ASL without understanding its rules probably would not be enough of a basis, for most, to go on and learn another language formally.

COMMUNICATING WITH DEAF CHILDREN

To date, all our efforts have focused on formal efforts to "teach" English to deaf children. In my view, this is a guaranteed road to failure. It is necessary to take a lesson from the real world of life and apply it to the lives of deaf children.

In the first place, most deaf children in residential schools for the deaf have seemed to graduate with a poor command of English, but an excellent ability to communicate fully with other deaf persons. We used to say that they have learned 'sign language'. Now we say that they learned American Sign Language. We used to say that 'sign language' was an inferior form of English because it was used by deaf people. Now we admit that they have learned a language although one that is a mystery for most of us hearing people. It is good that they have learned a language, but it is not so good that they have not mastered English, since English is still the language of education, of commerce, and of the greater society.

I recall that, when I was serving as Executive Secretary of the North Carolina Association of the Deaf, I would explain something or make a report or whatever. I signed because, after all, nearly everyone else in the meeting was deaf. When I finished with what I was saying, a deaf friend, now deceased, would then get up and tell the people what I had just said. I signed according to the rules of the language I knew -- English. Most of the people were not able to decode what I had said, so he translated my English order signing into ASL. That brought home, again, to me the obvious fact that English was not a language these folks had mastered.

In my years of acquaintance with deaf people, I quickly learned that ability to use English and levels of intelligence were not related for deaf people. All one has to do is think about various retarded people one knows and see how seriously retarded one has to be before spoken language does not develop to a very high level. Deaf people tend to be as intelligent or unintelligent as people with normal hearing. The fact that they may not be able to handle English really has nothing or very little to do with intellectual ability.

Why, then, is it so difficult for deaf persons to master English? The reason is simple. The language simply is not accessible to them.

Since it is not accessible to them, it is necessary to make it accessible to them. We have pretty well understood that for a long time. That is the reason we "teach" it in school. That is also the reason special 'oral' schools such as the Clarke School for the Deaf in Massachusetts or the Lexington School for the Deaf in New York City were organized. If deaf children are in a setting where all the people around them speak so that the children may see their speech, they will be able to learn the language of our society -- English. All well and good in theory. But the practical reality, in my experience, is that the majority of deaf persons do not have the ability (and it does seem to be an innate ability) to speechread (or, lipread if one prefers that term).

Since being deaf means being unable to hear, perhaps the solution lay in enhancing their hearing through the use of amplification. Amplification was the process of fitting deaf children with hearing aids and the equipping of classrooms with an amplifier with headsets connected so that the teacher's speech would be made louder for the children. Such equipment as the group systems and the individual aids was continually improved in the hope that the children would be able to benefit auditorially. So, most, if not all, schools for deaf children installed amplification systems, but the end result was the same---the deaf children still could not hear well enough to understand the amplified speech and, as a result, continued to be denied an opportunity to acquire English. The Verbotonal Method, imported from Yugoslavia, was interesting, but not much better.

Enter Cued Speech, an oral system utilizing hand shapes and positions to indicate speech phoneme groups. A hand shape used in conjunction with a speech phoneme allows the recipient to decide which of three disparate consonants is being spoken, and placement of the hand around the lower face represents the vowel sound being spoken. Hence, a word with four phonemic elements and one vowel sound would require four hand shapes and one particular position of the hand.

With cueing, speech in theory should become more understandable. This proved to be true. The net result seems to be that a good speechreader became a better speechreader because of the added information provided through cueing. By the same token, a lousy speechreader (which is what most deaf persons seem to be) became a better lousy speechreader. The same thing necessary for success in an 'oral' school, talent for speechreading, still seems to be the key to success under a Cued Speech system.

The most recent developmental effort to actually reverse deafness has been the cochlear implant (CI). The early results seem to be that many deaf children are able to benefit from the CI to the point that they are developing speech and, since the speech is English, moving toward a command of the English language. English is being made accessible for them.

COMMUNICATING WITH DEAF CHILDREN

Of course, all these special efforts before CIs sounded good to parents and received great support. How many parents were told that their children would learn to speak, and later learned a sad, hard truth? An advantage, too, was that we, the hearing people around the deaf children, didn't have to do much different in order to provide an enhanced setting for the children. Keep this point in mind.

Success in learning ASL for deaf children and failure in learning English for deaf children seem to be prime descriptors for what happens in schools for deaf children. Why is there success in the one language and not in the other? The answer is so simple, yet it seems to have evaded the field of education for deaf children for, lo, these many years. The one ingredient making all the difference in learning as opposed to being unable to learn is just simply *total accessibility*. For the deaf child without a CI, accessibility depends upon the visual sense, as opposed to the auditory sense for normally hearing children. ASL is totally visual and totally accessible to the deaf child. Too, ASL is the language used in an environment that is exclusively ASL; there are no competing languages to confuse the child. Based on my approximately 45 years of experience in a number of schools and programs for deaf children, it appears to me that spoken English simply is not sufficiently accessible for most deaf children. So-called "Signed English" (signing according to the rules of English), while totally visual and totally accessible, is not, strictly speaking, totally English, because too many words and parts of words are not signed by most persons using this communication modality. Therefore, the child is not in a situation where English is totally accessible.

Some systems of 'manual English', such as Signed (or Signing) Exact English (SEE), do provide complete English visually when executed correctly. I have heard reports of success using such a system. However, where one of the 'manual English' systems are used and ASL is also used in the child's presence, the child will be confused because so many of the 'manual English' signs come from ASL. We cannot expect the child to be able to discriminate between, for example, SEE and ASL, since the child is learning. It would be like using the French vocabulary while speaking French to a child and using the same vocabulary while following the rules for English. There has to be a clear difference between the two languages, and the vocabulary is clearly different for French and English.

The keys to learning a language, any language, are accessibility and consistency. Accessibility means that the language is in a form the child is able to understand. If the child has normal hearing, speech is an accessible modality for the child. If the child is deaf, the modality has to be manual so that it becomes visually accessible to the child (even deaf children who are able to speechread will benefit from the manual modality). Additionally, the language has to be consistently the same language. If we want the child to learn English, English is what we must use. If we want the child to learn Spanish, the language we must use is Spanish.

I am an English-speaking, -reading, and -writing person by virtue of the fact that I grew up, during my early years, my preschool years, in an environment that was totally English and totally accessible to me because I have normal hearing and reasonably normal intelligence. The key to English learning for a deaf child is precisely the same. The language (English) must be used in an exclusively English environment ***and*** it must be totally accessible to the child. For the deaf child, accessibility means a manual modality as opposed to an auditory modality for the normally hearing child.

If manual representation of English is the answer for the deaf child, why don't we simply adopt SEE or another similar system? There are several reasons. In the first place, it really doesn't make too much sense to bastardize a perfectly good language -- ASL -- by utilizing and modifying its vocabulary and applying a set of rules that do not apply to the language. This would be much like trying to teach Spanish by using its rules but using a German vocabulary. It simply will not work.

In the second place, ASL is a perfectly good and useful tool for the deaf community. It would make no sense to destroy a language used by so many people simply because we want deaf children to learn English. In addition, it would amount to denying deaf children access to what many believe is a cultural side to being deaf.

The answer is to use a manual modality *distinctly different* from ASL. Spoken languages are all distinctly different, auditorily. We hear the differences between and among languages and there is no confusion. English, for the deaf child, similarly, must be distinctly different from ASL, yet be produced in a manual modality. It would be too difficult a task to devise signs distinctly different from ASL signs for English words and, in any case, would probably result in total confusion for the deaf child. There is only one other manual modality available that will enable the deaf child to learn English in the "normal" way, and that manual modality is fingerspelling.

Fingerspelling has been around, probably as long as signing has, at least in educational settings. In the United States, for example, fingerspelling without signing was the method used at the Rochester (N.Y.) School for the Deaf from the late nineteenth century until around the 1940s. By all accounts, the method proved to be quite successful in terms of the level of English literacy acquired by the students who graduated from the school. In addition to the requirement that all employees at the school had to fingerspell, the entire school environment, indoors and out-of-doors, was labeled. The method was, of course, termed “The Rochester Method." This is the only instance of fingerspelling as the sole manual representation of English in the entire school environment. Ultimately, the method was abandoned apparently because of the demand for the strictly “oral method” during the children's early school years. Predictably, English literacy declined dramatically. Where English had been 100% accessible to deaf children by virtue of everyone in the school environment fingerspelling, it now became accessible only to those children who had a talent for speechreading. Without fingerspelling, most of the children were now denied an English environment and, hence, failed to acquire command of English. Literacy in English was now the exception to the rule.

More recently, fingerspelling was tried at the New Mexico School for the Deaf during the time I was a teacher there. Interestingly, young normally hearing children picked up fingerspelling in very short order. It seems that parents would bring their young children with them to the school during the time that they (the parents of young deaf children at the school) were being taught to fingerspell. The children were tended to in a corner of the room in which instructions were going on. No attempt was made to teach the children to fingerspell. Yet, in a matter of a few weeks they were fingerspelling amongst themselves.

Several years later, while I was teaching at the University of Tennessee, the superintendent of the Tennessee School for the Deaf decreed one year that henceforth all manual communication was to be in the form of fingerspelling. Needless to say, the dictum was pretty well ignored with the older children, but was implemented in the Primary Department which, at the time, was strictly "oral." Near the end of the first year, the supervising teacher took me aside and said, "I would never have believed it if I hadn't seen it with my own eyes. It really works." This was totally unsolicited, and the lady who said it had been an avowed "oralist" for about 30 years!

Still, ***fingerspelling without the use of any signs*** has not found favor with educators as a way to instill English in deaf children. One reason for this is that it is too "slow." This is sheer nonsense! What people probably really mean when they say that it is too slow is that it is too slow for them to use. Speech is much faster than fingerspelling and so is signing. Besides that, speech is easier for us hearing people to use, and signing is lots more fun. Neither of those reasons is good enough to deny deaf children an opportunity to learn the language of the greater society, the language of education, the language of commerce in this country. Our responsibility as adults, whether parents or teachers or others concerned and connected with the development of deaf children, is to meet the needs of the child ***on his/her terms!*** His/her terms are not auditory- nor speech-based.

All my teaching life in schools for deaf children seemed to be centered around teaching the children according to our preferences as normally hearing persons. The emphasis has always been on our communicating in a way that was comfortable for us. Thus, in some schools, we signed in the classroom and did so according to the rules for English. In other schools, there was no signing permitted in the classroom and the child was expected to learn through oral means. The child, not having a voice in the matter, had to struggle and suffer because things could only be done on our (the adult normally hearing persons responsible for their education) terms. No wonder that we failed so badly. We expected the child to learn and achieve on our terms, and when the child failed, it was "because the child did not try hard enough." The fact that we expected results in English, yet did not make it possible for the child to master English, never entered into the equation. Failure was always the child's fault.

All we really had to do was take a lesson from our own lives, understand how and why we mastered English, and apply that lesson to our work with deaf children. Is it too late? Could we not restructure our environments so that we could provide the deaf child with an English environment that is totally accessible to him?

I don't want to end this without making one more point. We need to provide ***two completely separate language environments*** for deaf children. In each environment, one or the other language must be used exclusively in the modality that will provide 100% accessibility for the deaf child. In one environment(s), ASL and only ASL. In a second environment(s), fingerspelled English and only fingerspelled English, with the spoken form encouraged, but not required, in order to promote whatever speechreading capability a child may have.

How should the environments be determined? A lot depends upon the physical layout of the school itself and whether a child is a residential or day student. The logical thing might seem to be that the school building should be an English environment and that outside the school building should be the ASL environment. Logic, I would be very much afraid, would probably not be the way to decide. Suffice it to say that the situation of the children would need to be studied and a sensible decision made as where and how the English and ASL environments should be set up.

With an approach that "sections off" environments for the child, we can virtually guarantee every deaf child will grow up as a bilingual person perfectly at home, hopefully, in ASL and in English. One final point, too. By the time a child is 12 or 13, you may be assured that the child will have learned, in a natural way, the language(s) we refer to as the child's "first" or "primary" language(s). For the deaf child, the goal would be to have acquired two "first/primary" languages -- ASL and English.

[Contributed by Glenn T. Lloyd, EdD.]

Also available from Kodiak Media Group . . .

AN INTELLECTUAL LOOK AT ASL

Edited by Tom Bertling

"[Editor] Tom Bertling and his contributors, all highly regarded professionals, offer startling and substantial evidence, scientifically and logically and yet reasonably, to prove that the Bilingual/Bicultural ASL track does not produce educated, literate children. . . . an indispensable, convincing and definitive appeal to sanity . . . a stern warning. . ." -Arnold B. Adelman, Director
SPEECH & HEARING FND./MA

"Tom Bertling keeps the pot boiling in this lively discussion of ASL and its place in bilingual education of deaf and hard of hearing students . . ." -Gerilee Gustason, PhD, Professor
SAN JOSE STATE UNIVERSITY

"Once again, Editor Tom Bertling has done a remarkable job. . . Highly educational and written in an easy to read style . . . vital . . ."
-Warren T. Hanna, Exec. Director
HRD. OF HEARING ADVOCATES

". . . one of the best things to happen in the world of people with hearing disabilities. . . . outstanding . . ."
-Richard Roehm III, Activist/Editor
DEAF WATCH NEWSLETTER

"Critically important reading for educators, administrators, parents . . ." -James A. Cox, Editor-in-Chief
MIDWEST BOOK REVIEW

"Throughout the concise book are many, many quotable and revealing points . . ." -Stan Foran, Editor
CONTACT *(IRELAND)*

". . . honest discourse on ASL and education of the deaf. . ."
-Prof. Frances M. Parsons, Author
GALLAUDET UNIVERSITY

TO ORDER THIS BOOK SEE ORDER FORM ON PAGE 112

ASL: SHATTERING THE MYTH

Edited by Tom Bertling

" . . . sounds an alarm to all parents and teachers of deaf children . . ."
-Ed. Scouten, Distinguish. Educator
GALLAUDET UNIVERSITY, NTID

". . . a "wake-up call" to the guardians of education -- teachers and administrators . . ."
-Dr. Robert F. Panara, Prof. Emeritus
NTID/ROCH. INST. OF TECH.

"[Editor] Tom Bertling has done an excellent job . . ."
-Paulette R. Caswell, M.S.-TESL, J.D.
***USC** (PhD Program)*

". . . indispensable, highly recommended reading for educators, administrators . . ."
-James A. Cox, Editor-in-Chief
MIDWEST BOOK REVIEW

". . . written by respected deaf scholars . . . a balanced view of the current atmosphere of academic repression, especially at Gallaudet University."
-Thomas J. Balkany, MD, FACS
UNIVERSITY OF MIAMI

"Tom Bertling provides a valuable service to all educators, parents of deaf children . . ."
-Arnold B. Adelman, Director
SPEECH & HEARING FND/MA

". . . a must have, must read, must share book."
-Nancy Tamburello, Interpreter
INDEPENDENT PUBLISHER

". . . understandable by the layperson, yet in-depth enough to be of interest to the scholar."
Sara Marcus, MLS, Librarian
HEARING REHAB QUARTERLY

". . . thought-provoking . . . mandatory reading for . . . a balanced understanding . . ."
-Stan Foran, Editor
***CONTACT** (IRELAND)*

TO ORDER THIS BOOK SEE ORDER FORM ON PAGE 112

A CHILD SACRIFICED

TO THE DEAF CULTURE

INSTRUCTIONAL-CLASSROOM EDITION

By Tom Bertling

What others are saying about this book . . .

". . . A masterpiece . . . gripping . . . powerful . . . the author's outstanding legacy to the world."

-Prof. Frances Parsons, Author
GALLAUDET UNIVERSITY

". . . opened my eyes to a new perspective on cultural deafness...this information is vital to parents . . ."

--Thomas J. Balkany, MD, FACS
Hotchkiss Distinguished Professor
UNIVERSITY OF MIAMI

"One hopes this book will be read by members of the deaf community with an eye towards critical self evaluation."

-Dr. Lloyd Lamb, Book Reviewer
AMERICAN JOURNAL OF OTOLOGY

"Tom Bertling swims where few dare to tread . . ."

-Paula Bonillas, Publisher and Editor
HEARING HEALTH

"A remarkable new book . . . at first hand, the author explains the motives of the deaf leaders . . . should be required reading . . ."

-Otto J. Menzel, Ph.D., Editor
LIFE AFTER DEAFNESS

". . . a heartfelt book . . . you'll be amazed . . ."

-Shawn Lovley, Book Reviewer
ALDA NEWS

NO DIGNITY FOR JOSHUA

By Tom Bertling

What others are saying about this book . . .

"Tom Bertling is the crusading knight who is challenging those fanatics, in defense of the coming generation of children who deserve a better fate than to be sacrificial pawns in a futile effort to preserve what those fanatics call "culture." If this be "genocide," make the most of it!"

-Otto J. Menzel, Ph.D., Editor
LIFE AFTER DEAFNESS

"Following the success of "A Child Sacrificed . . . ," Tom Bertling's second book "No Dignity for Joshua" continues the revelation by a "Deaf of Deaf" insider . . . His insights into the realities of the Deaf community, especially regarding sexual abuse of children, are disturbing. . . . Bertling's writing skills evidence the advantage of early exposure to hearing and even a short period of mainstreamed oral education. Tom Bertling is the conscience of the Deaf-World."

-Thomas J. Balkany, MD, FACS, FAAP
Hotchkiss Distinguished Professor
UNIVERSITY OF MIAMI

"From the oppression of deaf children to the bashing of Miss America, Bertling dissects the inner workings of a small but powerful group who wield tremendous influence over our nation's culturally deaf community. It is amazing to me how all this explosive material Bertling covers has missed the scrutiny of the mainstream press!"

-Paula Bonillas, Editor and Publisher
HEARING HEALTH

"The world needs more people like Tom Bertling to advocate on behalf of saving a crucial language for the deaf -- ENGLISH."

-Frances M. Parsons, Author
GALLAUDET UNIVERSITY

USE ORDER FORM ON THE NEXT PAGE